Discovering My Vocation in Christ

A Core Course of the School of Leadership

Church of the Nazarene

Mesoamerica Region

Mónica Mastronardi de Fernández

Discovering my vocation in Christ

A book in the "School of Leadership" series.
Core Level Course

Author: Mónica Mastronardi de Fernández

Spanish Editor: Dr. Mónica E. Mastronardi de Fernández
Spanish Reviewer: Dr. Rubén Fernández
Translator: Alejandra Martinez de Riddell
Reviewer: Dorothy Bullon / Shelley J. Webb

Material produced by EDUCATION AND CLERGY DEVELOPMENT
of the Church of the Nazarene, Mesoamerica Region. www.edunaz.org
Mailing Address: PO Box 3977 - 1000 San José, Costa Rica, Central América.
Phone (506) 2285-0432 / 0423 - Email: EL@mesoamericaregion.org

Publisher and Distributor: Asociación Región Mesoamérica
Av. 12 de Octubre Plaza Victoria Locales 5 y 6
Pueblo Nuevo Hato Pintado, Ciudad de Panamá
Tel. (507) 203-3541
E-mail: literatura@mesoamericaregion.org

Copyright © 2017 - All rights reserved.
Reproduction whole or in part, by any means, without written permission from
Education and Clergy Development of the Church of the Nazarene, Mesoamerica Region is prohibited.
www.mesoamericaregion.org

All Biblical quotations are from the New International Version-2011, unless otherwise noted.

Design: Juan Manuel Fernandez (www.juanfernandez.ga)
Cover image: D'Angelo Favata
Cover images and interiors of the covers used with permission under license by Creative Commons.

Digital printing

Table of Contents

Lesson 1	Discovering My Spiritual Gifts	9
Lesson 2	Pastoral and Leadership Gifts	19
Lesson 3	Teaching and Preaching Gifts	27
Lesson 4	Evangelism and Spiritual Counseling Gifts	35
Lesson 5	Gifts of Compassion and Service	43
Lesson 6	Gifts Related to Cross-Cultural Ministry	51
Lesson 7	Gifts of Creative Arts and Communications	59
Lesson 8	What is My Role in the Body of Christ?	67

Introduction

The book series **School of Leadership** is designed with the purpose of providing a tool to the church for formation, education and training of its members to actively integrate into Christian service the gifts and calling (vocation) they have received from the Lord.

Each book provides study materials for one course in the **School of Leadership** program offered by the theological Institutions of the Mesoamerica Region of the Church of the Nazarene. These institutions include: IBN (Coban, Guatemala); STN (Guatemala City); SENAMEX (Mexico City); SENDAS (San Jose, Costa Rica); SND (Santo Domingo, Dominican Republic); and SETENAC (Havana, Cuba). A number of leaders from these schools (presidents, directors, vice presidents and directors of decentralized academic studies) actively participated in the program design.

The **School of Leadership** has five core courses that are common to all ministries, and six specialized courses for each ministry area, at the end of which, the respective theological institution awards the student a certificate (or diploma) in Specialized Ministry.

The overall objective of the **School of Leadership** is "to work with the local church in equipping the saints for the work of the ministry establishing a solid biblical and theological foundation and developing them through the practice of exercising their gifts for service in the local congregation and society as a whole." The specific objectives of this program are threefold:

- Develop the ministerial gifts of the local congregation.
- Multiply service ministries in the church and community.
- Raise awareness of the vocation of professional ministry in its diverse forms.

We thank Dr. Monica Mastronardi de Fernandez for her dedication as General Editor of the project, and the Regional Coordinators of Ministries and the team of writers and designers who collaborated to publish these books. We are equally grateful to the teachers who will share these materials. They will make a difference in the lives of thousands of people in the Mesoamerica Region and beyond.

Finally, we thank Dr. L. Carlos Saenz, Mesoamerica Regional Director, for his continued support in this work, which is the result of his conviction that the church must be holistically equipped.

We pray for God's blessing for all the disciples whose lives and Christian service will be enriched by these books.

Dr. Ruben E. Fernandez
Theological Education Coordinator
Mesoamerica Region

What Is the School of Leadership?

The School of Leadership is an educational program for lay ministry in different specialties to engage in the mission of the local church. This program is administered by the Theological Institutions of the Church of the Nazarene in the Mesoamerica Region and taught both at these institutions and in the local churches enrolled in the program.

Who Can Benefit from the School of Leadership?

It is for all the members of the Church of the Nazarene who have participated in Levels B and C of the discipleship program, and who, with all their heart, wish to discover their gifts and serve God in His work.

The Plan ABCDE

In order to contribute to the formation of the members of their churches, the Church of the Nazarene in the Mesoamerica Region has adopted the plan of discipleship ABCDE, and since 2001 began publishing materials for each of these levels. The School of Leadership is Level D of the ABCDE discipleship plan and is designed for those who have been through previous levels of discipleship.

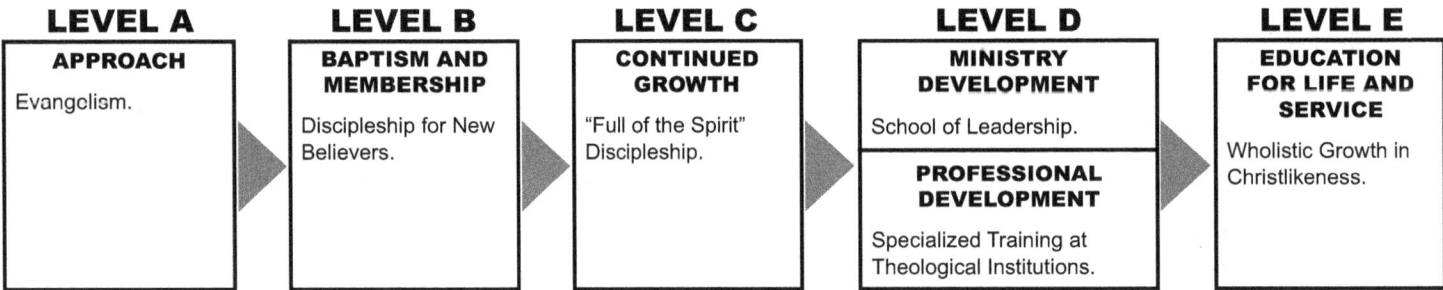

In the Church of the Nazarene, we believe making disciples in the image of Christ in the nations is the foundation of missionary work and the responsibility of leadership (Ephesians 4: 7-16). The work of discipleship is continuous and dynamic; therefore, the disciple never stops growing in the likeness of his Lord. This growth, when healthy, occurs in all dimensions: the individual dimension (spiritual growth), the corporate dimension (joining the congregation), the holiness in life dimension (progressive transformation of our being and doing according to the model of Jesus Christ) and the service dimension (investing our lives in ministry).

Dr. Monica Mastronardi de Fernandez
Managing Editor, The School of Leadership Book Series

How Do I Use This Book?

This book contains eight lessons of the School of Leadership program, along with activities and final evaluation of the course.

How are the contents of this book organized?

Each of the eight lessons of this book contains the following:

➢ **Objectives:** These are the learning objectives the student is expected to understand at the end of the lesson.

➢ **Main Ideas:** A summary of the key teachings of the lesson.

➢ **Development of Lesson:** This is the largest section because it is the development of the contents of the lesson. The lessons have been written so that the book can be the teacher, and for that reason the contents have been written in a dynamic form and in simple language with contemporary ideas.

➢ **Notes and Comments:** The information in the margins is intended to clarify terms and provide notes that complement or extend the content of the lesson.

➢ **Questions:** Sometimes questions are included in the margin that the teacher can use to introduce or reinforce a lesson topic.

➢ **What did we learn?:** The box at the end of the lesson development section provides a brief summary of the lesson.

➢ **Activities:** This is a page at the end of each lesson that contains learning activities, for individuals or groups, on the subject studied. The estimated time for implementation in class is 20 minutes.

➢ **Final evaluation of the course:** This is the last page of the book and once completed the student must remove it from the book and hand it in to a course instructor. The final evaluation should take about 15 minutes.

How long is each course?

The courses are designed for 12 hours of class over 8 ninety-minute sessions. Each institution and each church or local theological study center will coordinate days and times of the classes. Within this hour and a half the teacher or the teachers should include time for the activities contained in the book.

What is the role of the student?

The student is responsible for the following:

1. Enroll on time for the course.
2. Buy the book and study each lesson before class time.
3. Arrive for class on time.
4. Participate in class activities.
5. Participate in practical ministry in the local church outside of class.
6. Complete and submit the final evaluation to the teacher.

What is the role of the teacher of the course?

The professors and teachers for the School of Leadership courses are pastors and laity committed to the mission and ministry of the church and preferably have experience in the ministry they teach. The Director and/or the School of Leadership at the local church (or theological institution) invites their participation and their functions are the following:

1. Be well prepared by studying the book's content and scheduling the use of class time. When studying the lesson, you should have on hand the Bible and a dictionary. Although the lessons are written using simple language, it is recommended that you "translate" what you consider difficult in order to help the students understand. In other words, use terms that they can better understand.

2. Ensure that the students are studying the material in the book and achieving the learning objectives.

3. Plan and accompany students in the activities of ministerial practice. The local pastor and the director of the respective ministry must schedule these activities. These activities should not take away from class time.

4. Take daily attendance and grades in the class report form. The final average will be the result demonstrated by the student in the following activities:

   a. Class work
   b. Participation in ministerial practice outside of class
   c. Final evaluation

5. At the end of the course, collect the evaluation sheets and hand them in with the form "Class Report" to the local School of Leadership director. Do this after totaling the averages and verifying that all data is complete on the form.

6. Professors and teachers should not add tasks or reading assignments apart from the contents of the book. They should be creative in the design of the learning activities and in planning ministry activities outside the classroom according to the reality of their local church and its context.

How do I teach a class?

We recommend using a 90-minute class session as follows:

- **5 minutes:** Review the topic of the previous lesson and pray together.

- **30 minutes:** Review and discuss the lesson. We recommend using an outline, chalkboard, cardboard or other available materials, using dynamic learning activities and visual media such as graphics, drawings, objects, pictures, questions, assigning students to submit parts of the lesson, and so on. We do not recommend lecturing or having the teacher reread the lesson content.

- **5 minutes:** Break either in the middle of class or when it is convenient.

- **20 minutes:** Work on activities in the book. This can be done at the beginning, middle or end of the review, or you can complete the activities as you proceed in accordance with the issues as it relates to them.

• **20 minutes:** Discussion about the students' ministry practice that they currently do and that they will do. At the beginning of the course you will need to present the schedule to the students so that they can make arrangements to attend the ministry practice. In the classes when the students discuss their ministry practice, the conversation should be focused on what they learned, including their successes and their errors, as well as the difficulties they encountered.

• **10 minutes:** Prayer for the issues arising from the practice (challenges, people, problems, goals, gratitude for the results, among others).

How do I implement the final course evaluation?

Allocate 15 minutes of time during the last class meeting for the course evaluation. If necessary, students may consult their books and Bibles. Final evaluations are designed to be an activity to reinforce what was learned in class and not a repetition of the contents of the book. The purpose of this assessment is to measure the understanding and evaluation of the student concerning the class topics, their spiritual growth, their progress in the commitment to the mission of the church and their progress in ministerial experience.

Ministerial Practice Activities

The following are suggested activities for ministerial practice outside of class. The list below includes several ideas to help teachers, pastors, directors of local School of Leadership groups and local ministry directors. From the list you can choose the activity best suited to the contextual situation and the local church ministry, or replace these with others according to the needs and possibilities of your context.

We recommend having at least three ministerial activities per course. You can put the whole class to work on a project or assign group tasks according to interests, gifts and abilities. It is advisable to involve students in a variety of new ministry experiences.

Suggested Ministry Activities for Discovering My Vocation in Christ

Ministerial Specialty	*Suggested Activities for Practical Ministry*
PASTORAL AND LEADERSHIP GIFTS Leadership, Administration, Wisdom, Pastor	1. Plan a breakfast with the pastor and several church leaders so the students can ask questions to the leaders about their calling and their responsibilities. 2. Serve as the pastor´s (or another leader's) assistant for a week to assist them with their assigned ministry.
TEACHING AND PREACHING GIFTS Discernment, Knowledge Teaching, Prophecy	1. Analyze the sermon to evaluate the topic and how it was presented. In what ways could it be improved? 2. Design a survey to find out what people are learning in the church. What do they remember of the teaching through sermons or Sunday School? How are they applying it in their lives?
EVANGELISM AND SPIRITUAL COUNSELING GIFTS Faith, Miracles and Healing, Exhortation, Evangelism, Intercession	1. Invite people who have experience in these ministries to share their testimony and advice, and answer questions from students. 2. Support a church evangelistic project by doing personal evangelism, visiting homes or other similar projects.
GIFTS OF COMPASSION AND SERVICE Hospitality, Service and Support, Generosity, Compassion	1. Visit a hospital, prison, orphanage, an elderly care center or home, or another such location to meet spiritual needs and hand out materials. 2. Visit community centers or invite their leaders so as to learn from their work.
GIFTS RELATED TO CROSS-CULTURAL MINISTRY Languages, Apostle, Missionary	1. Assist with a cross-cultural ministry for a week as helpers. 2. Do a group research project on the status of the Christian missions in the world by using the Internet.
GIFTS OF CREATIVE ARTS AND COMMUNICATIONS Writing, Music, Skilled Labor and Arts, Communications	1. Participate in a mission project or Work and Witness team to fill a need in the church or the community. 2. Work in a decorating project for a special activity at church, design a video to watch in a service, or design a printed newsletter on a special topic (for example, a documentary on the practical ministry realized by the groups of this course).

Lesson 1

Discovering My Spiritual Gifts

Objectives

- Define spiritual gift, ministry and vocation.
- Understand when spiritual gifts are received.
- Identify gifts through a test.

Main Ideas

- All Christians have a vocation, gifts, and are called to the ministry.
- Gifts are varied and necessary for the mission of the church.
- When we discover our gifts, we can be trained for service.

Introduction

In 1996, a Work and Witness team from the United States went to Puerto Rico to build a chapel, and they stayed next to a house where they raised roosters. It was difficult to sleep at night due the constant "singing" which is typical of these birds. Then they began to wonder why roosters have this annoying habit, and why do they crow constantly. One member of the group answered the question, "Why do roosters crow?" saying, "Because they do it well."

This simple story teaches us a great truth: God wants His children to serve Him doing what they have been gifted to do, and doing it well. We do not all need to be important theologians and preachers to serve our Father. God has given one or more gifts to all Christians to use for His service. He only asks us to invest what He has given us. God calls us to fulfill the vocation in Christ for which we have been created.

What Is a Spiritual Gift?

Spiritual gifts are abilities that the Holy Spirit gives to members of the church so as to serve according to His calling.

Spiritual gifts are given by the Holy Spirit.

A spiritual gift is the ability or capacity received from God through the Holy Spirit to perform a Christian service. Some gifts include teaching, providing for the needs of others, healing the sick, among others (1 Corinthians 12:4, Romans 12:6, 1 Corinthians 12:31-13:13).

What Is Ministry?

Ministry is all the work we do to serve God and others.

The term ministry encompasses all work assignments in the church. In the New Testament, ministry was a "function" that all brothers and sisters took part in, that is, all the disciples participated in the task of presenting Christ according to their gifts and capabilities.

Over the centuries this function was centralized in one person: the priest or pastor, and this affected the mission of the church, leaving the members separated from ministry. However, in the Bible, the term "ministry" applies to many more functions than any one person (Senior Pastor) can perform.

We are thankful that in our time, Christians are rediscovering the New Testament principles regarding the priesthood of "all believers" (1 Peter 2:5-9). In Ephesians 4, Paul teaches that God's call to ministry is for all believers regardless of their age, sex, marital status, social class, race or educational background, and they share the following privileges by the grace of God:

- They are called.
- They must walk worthy of their "calling."
- They have a "vocation."
- They have the same Spirit that unites them.
- They have gifts.
- They are ministers and have a ministry.
- Some of them are set apart for roles of spiritual leadership.

When every believer serves according to his or her gifts, it prevents other members from being overloaded with tasks and feeling exhausted.

Paul teaches that there are special leadership ministries: apostle, prophet, evangelist, pastor and teacher (Ephesians 4:11), but these are not the only ones who have a ministry in the church, since God's purpose is to equip "all" Christians for the work of ministry (v. 12). The verb "equip" refers to providing education and training for each member of the Body of Christ in order that they might serve God and their neighbors, according to the gifts received from the Holy Spirit.

What Is Vocation?

There is only one vocation in the life of a Christian.

Vocation is the inclination placed in the heart of Christians by the Holy Spirit for a profession or job where they can invest their lives in serving God and their neighbor.

In the early centuries of Church history, vocation was understood as the inclination to the work of ministry or a religious calling. Afterwards the term was secularized, in other words, it was applied to other non-religious professions and trades, such as, the vocation of a teacher, doctor, mason, and so on. Over time a division arose between a "secular" and a "religious" vocation. And so, a Christian could have a job to make a living (secular vocation) and, at the same time, have a ministry in the church where he or she served God. This leads to a division between the two vocations, and permanent tensions as to which should receive more energy, time, and skills.

When believers use their gifts, there is more joy in the congregation and many more ministries of service to the community.

Lesson 1 - Discovering My Spiritual Gifts

Spiritual gifts are not given to satisfy our own needs, but to meet the needs of others.

Given this confusion, we must return to the Biblical meaning of the term. Everyone has a vocation, that is a purpose or mission for which God gave them life. This vocation is performed in everything a person does, whether in church, at work, at school, or with their family, etc. Christians never cease to serve God. In the Bible, life, service, and worship go together and are inseparable.

So a person can work as a baker, and because he has the gift of service, he could be a steward in the local church. When he is kneading bread to feed the people, he is not just doing it for a paycheck, but as a service to his Lord, sharing not only bread, but also the bread of life which is Christ Jesus. In this way, any occupation or profession becomes, for the Christian, a ministry in a place where we fulfill our vocation.

How and When Do You Receive a Spiritual Gift?

The gifts are received at the time of being born again.

Do not confuse gifts with talents. Talents are natural abilities given at birth. In some cases, these abilities are transformed into gifts by the Holy Spirit.

Spiritual gifts are given to new believers at the time they receive new life in Christ, at their conversion. It is then that we are born into the family of God and the Holy Spirit comes to dwell in our lives teaching us and guiding us in the process of growing into the image of Christ. In this first "baptism" of the Spirit, gifts are given in order to serve God and others. As he or she grows, the believer learns to identify his or her vocation in Christ, the ministry for which life has been given by the Father.

In the church in Corinth there were many relationship problems between brothers and sisters in the faith. This was because they still lived governed by their own selfish desires and had not experienced the fullness of the Holy Spirit. This church is praised by the apostle for the wealth of gifts they had, but he warned them about the danger of implementing the gifts without perfect love. Instead of edifying the church, the Corinthians' gifts were destroying it.

No matter how many gifts we have, we must seek this second work of grace, the fullness of the Spirit, in order to use them in a right attitude of helpful love.

How Many Gifts Are There?

Spiritual gifts should not be confused with the fruit of the Spirit. Gifts enable us to "do" something, while the fruit of the Spirit imparts the qualities of the character of Christ: love, joy, peace, patience, kindness, goodness, faithfulness, gentleness, and self-control (Galatians 5:22).

There are as many gifts as there are needs in the church and community.

In the New Testament there are several lists of gifts:
- 1 Corinthians 12:8-10
- Romans 12
- 1 Corinthians 12:28-30
- Ephesians 4:11
- 1 Corinthians 13
- 1 Peter 5:1

School of Leadership - Discovering My Vocation in Christ

There are other gifts listed in 1Timothy 3:11, 5:9, 6:12 and 2 Timothy 2:22.

The gifts mentioned in these passages are the following: apostle, prophet, teacher, miracles, healing, tongues, interpretation, knowledge, faith, discernment of spirits, insight, wisdom, support, administration, martyrdom, giving, mercy, service, leadership, ministry with women, with widows, and others. Looking at the list of gifts that are mentioned in the New Testament, we can draw the following conclusions.

1. There are gifts that appear together such as being an elder, bishop, pastor, and teacher (Ephesians 4:11, 1 Timothy 5:17). This indicates that there are gifts that come together because they are required to perform certain ministerial roles. For example, a pastor must have the gift of teaching since one of his responsibilities is to edify believers in the Word.

2. The gifts are distributed to all Christians, not just to pastors and leaders. All who have received new life in Christ have at least one gift (1 Corinthians 7:7, Ephesians 4:7, 1 Peter 4:10 and Romans 12:3).

3. Ministry, which means service to God and others, is for everyone, not just for those with professional theological education.

4. Ministries involve working as a team. It requires a variety of gifts to lead local congregations, to open missionary fields, for theological education, for youth ministry, etc.

5. There is great diversity of gifts and ministries. This means that God is creative and wise in giving gifts to church members so that they may serve to meet the needs of their church and community.

In the activities section, there is a test included to help you to identify your gifts.

> Do not confuse a spiritual gift with ministerial function or position. For example, the gift of teaching is required for teachers; the gift of hospitality for hosts and hostesses; the gift of leadership, for coordinators of ministries.

A minister is one who serves God and people. Jesus taught that a servant attitude is needed to serve (Matthew 20:26-28).

What Did We Learn?

The spiritual gifts are abilities that the Holy Spirit distributes to members of the church to serve in His work. All Christians have the responsibility to discover their gifts, receive teaching and training from spiritual leaders, and give their lives serving their calling and vocation in Christ.

Lesson 1 - Discovering My Spiritual Gifts

Activities

Time 20'

INSTRUCTIONS:

STEP 1. Complete the Spiritual Gifts Test

Each of the 96 test questions describes activities. Evaluate each one according to your interest, whether you have practiced them or not, according the following scoring table:

0. No, this does not interest me (no matter if I have experienced it or not)
1. I have very little interest
2. I have some interest
3. I am more interested in this than others
4. Yes, this is what I enjoy (I would like to specialize in/dedicate myself to this)

QUESTIONS:

1. ___ Do I prefer to communicate in writing rather than talking?
2. ___ Do I usually take a step forward and assume leadership of a group where there is none?
3. ___ Do I tend to identify and go to people who are alone in services or church activities?
4. ___ Do I have the ability to recognize a big or small need and resolve it?
5. ___ Do I have the ability to organize ideas, people, and projects to fulfill a specific purpose?
6. ___ Do I have the ability to recognize when someone doesn't have a genuine spiritual life?
7. ___ Am I generally sure we can accomplish great things for the glory of God?
8. ___ Do I rejoice when I sing or play musical instruments during church services?
9. ___ Do I have the ability to learn languages?
10. ___ Has God done miracles and healings through my prayers?
11. ___ Do I have the ability to use my hands in designing and building things?
12. ___ Do I like the idea of using technology to communicate something?
13. ___ Do I consider giving money to the work of the church a privilege rather than a liability?
14. ___ When I see someone's need, am I moved by a desire to do something to help?
15. ___ Do I usually have insights to offer a useful solution when a problem arises?
16. ___ Do I investigate an issue to get the bottom of the truth?
17. ___ Do I rejoice in encouraging and giving comfort to those who are discouraged?
18. ___ Do I want to study scriptural topics thoroughly and share them with others?
19. ___ Am I passionate about helping others in their spiritual growth?
20. ___ Would I like to see there be a church in each community where people could congregate?
21. ___ Do I feel drawn to evangelize groups of marginalized or foreign people?

22 ___ Do I like listening to a sermon and thinking about how I could present that message?
23 ___ Do I rejoice being with those who are not Christians, hoping to talk about Jesus?
24 ___ When I hear news or a conversation about needs, do I feel burdened to pray?
25 ___ Do I know more vocabulary than most people my age and use words properly?
26 ___ Is it easy for me to ask others to help with or contribute to a project?
27 ___ Do I delight in assisting guests so that they feel comfortable in my home or at church?
28 ___ Do I delight in serving others, no matter if the task is simple or small?
29 ___ Am I very organized and plan the steps necessary to achieve an objective?
30 ___ Can I easily distinguish when a person speaks and acts truthfully or deceitfully?
31 ___ Am I a naturally motivated person?
32 ___ Do I like to express my feelings to God through song in my private worship?
33 ___ Do I like helping people with different languages to be able to communicate?
34 ___ When necessary, do I pray with faith waiting for God to work in a supernatural way?
35 ___ Do I enjoy doing crafts such as woodwork, painting, or sewing?
36 ___ Do I have the ability to use media such as audio, video, etc.?
37 ___ Do I financially support brothers and sisters in need by giving money when I can?
38 ___ Do I think it is worth investing my time to help people with their needs?
39 ___ Does God allow me to choose correctly between several options when others do not know what to do?
40 ___ Do I study hard issues in God's Word tirelessly until I find the answer?
41 ___ Do people often tell me their problems and I encourage them?
42 ___ Do I have the creativity to explain or illustrate complicated issues in a simple way?
43 ___ Do I feel compassion for people who have no shepherd?
44 ___ Would I be excited and willing to start a new church?
45 ___ Can I adapt easily to other cultures and lifestyles different from mine?
46 ___ Do I always talk about Christian principles, even if what I say is not popular?
47 ___ Would I like to be well trained to evangelize people?
48 ___ Do I believe that prayer is the most important thing Christians can do?
49 ___ When I read something written by someone else, do I realize if they are expressing themselves poorly?
50 ___ Can I guide a group of people to achieve a specific goal?
51 ___ Do I rejoice in getting to know new people and introducing them to a group?
52 ___ Can I be depended on to accomplish tasks in a given time?
53 ___ Is it easy for me to delegate and trust other people to do difficult tasks?
54 ___ Can I distinguish between right and wrong in complex spiritual matters more than others?
55 ___ Do I have confidence in God's faithfulness for the future, even in the midst of problems?
56 ___ Do I rejoice in singing and do some people say I have a good voice?
57 ___ Is it easy and natural for me to learn a language and use it to edify the lives of others?
58 ___ Does God regularly bring to my mind someone who is sick when I pray?
59 ___ Do I think it is very important that church buildings are in good condition?
60 ___ Can I write scripts for a play, radio, or television?

61 ___ Am I willing to deprive myself of something so as to give more generous offerings?

62 ___ Am I willing to sacrifice my time to meet the needs of others?

63 ___ Do people often seek my advice for their lives when they don't know what to do?

64 ___ If I have a question, do I seek information from different sources to find the answer?

65 ___ Am I bold about confronting another person in order to help them in their spiritual growth?

66 ___ Would I like to learn more about teaching techniques to teach God's word?

67 ___ Do I enjoy working with people, helping them to grow in their service to the Lord?

68 ___ Do I identify with church planters?

69 ___ Would I like to evangelize in a language, culture, and lifestyle different from mine?

70 ___ Am I driven by the desire to teach God's will for the lives of His children?

71 ___ Is it one of the happiest moments of my life when someone accepts Jesus as Savior?

72 ___ Is it natural for me to put the needs of others before mine when I pray?

73 ___ When I write, do I review the material to make sure it is clearly stated?

74 ___ Do people usually respect my opinions and follow my directions?

75 ___ Do I like to open my home to receive visitors?

76 ___ Do I rejoice in helping leaders in whatever they need and I am happy to meet that need?

77 ___ Do I feel comfortable making important decisions even under pressure?

78 ___ Do I easily identify when God's Word is wrongly interpreted and taught?

79 ___ When I pray, do I do it with faith and often see that God answers my prayers in amazing ways?

80 ___ Would I like to convey a message through a song so that others might be edified?

81 ___ Do I feel compassion for people who do not have Christian books and Bibles in their own language?

82 ___ When someone faces a difficult situation, do I encourage them and pray with them, asking for divine intervention?

83 ___ Do I like to use photography, painting, plays and other art forms to convey a message?

84 ___ Would I like to help others by teaching techniques to improve communication between people?

85 ___ When I give money to someone, am I one who does not expect a thank you or recognition in front of others?

86 ___ Do I have the ability to find resources so that needs can be met even when others give up?

87 ___ Do I have the ability to apply the principles of the Word to make decisions in my daily life?

88 ___ Do I devote a lot of time to identifying Biblical truths and principles and enjoy doing it?

89 ___ Do people feel comfortable telling me their problems?

90 ___ Are my thoughts organized when presenting Bible teaching to a group of people?

91 ___ Do I rejoice in giving spiritual guidance to people when they are experiencing problems?

92 ___ Would I like to form new groups of Christians in areas where there are not many churches?

93 ___ Am I willing to use my financial resources to go and serve the Lord in distant places?

94 ___ Is it relatively easy for me to apply the teachings of the Bible to today's situations?

95 ___ Do I have a lot of interest in leading others to become Christians?

96 ___ Is prayer my favorite ministry in the church and do I spend much of the time practicing it?

STEP 2: Add up the answers for the Spiritual Gifts Test

After completing the test, copy the results of each item in the "Table of Answers" (below). Then add the four digits scored horizontally and enter the result in the column "TOTAL."

Consider the following example:

RESULTS				TOTAL	GIFT
1. 2	25. 1	49. 1	73. 2	6	A
2. 4	26. 3	50. 2	74. 2	11	B

ANSWERS				TOTAL	GIFT
1.	25.	49.	73.		A. WRITING
2.	26.	50.	74.		B. LEADERSHIP
3.	27.	51.	75.		C. HOSPITALITY
4.	28.	52.	76.		D. SERVICE AND HELPING
5.	29.	53.	77.		E. ADMINISTRATION
6.	30.	54.	78.		F. DISCERNMENT
7.	31.	55.	79.		G. FAITH
8.	32.	56.	80.		H. MUSIC
9.	33.	57.	81.		I. LANGUAGES
10.	34.	58.	82.		J. MIRACLES AND HEALING
11.	35.	59.	83.		K. ARTS / SKILLED LABOR
12.	36.	60.	84.		L. COMMUNICATION
13.	37.	61.	85.		M. GENEROSITY
14.	38.	62.	86.		N. COMPASSION
15.	39.	63.	87.		O. WISDOM
16.	40.	64.	88.		P. KNOWLEDGE
17.	41.	65.	89.		Q. EXHORTATION
18.	42.	66.	90.		R. TEACHING
19.	43.	67.	91.		S. PASTOR
20.	44.	68.	92.		T. APOSTLE
21.	45.	69.	93.		U. MISSIONARY
22.	46.	70.	94.		V. PROPHECY
23.	47.	71.	95.		W. EVANGELISM
24.	48.	72.	96.		X. INTERCESSION

STEP 3: *Identify Your Ministerial Specialty*

INSTRUCTIONS

Your highest scores in the total column above indicate your STRONGEST GIFTS. Now find these gifts in your MINISTERIAL SPECIALTY.

MINISTERIAL SPECIALTIES

PASTORAL AND LEADERSHIP GIFTS	TEACHING AND PREACHING GIFTS	EVANGELISM AND SPIRITUAL COUNSELING GIFTS
Leadership Administration Wisdom Pastor (Lesson 2)	Discernment Knowledge Teaching Prophecy (Lesson 3)	Faith Miracles and Healing Exhortation Evangelism Intercession (Lesson 4)
GIFTS OF COMPASSION AND SERVICE	GIFTS RELATED TO CROSS-CULTURAL MINISTRY	GIFTS OF CREATIVE ARTS AND COMMUNICATIONS
Hospitality Service and Support Generosity Compassion (Lesson 5)	Languages Apostle Missionary (Lesson 6)	Writing Music Skilled Labor and Arts Communications (Lesson 7)

The next six lessons will include a study of each of these groups of gifts. A deeper study of your strongest gifts will be helpful in confirming and knowing how to start serving in your church.

Lesson 2

PASTORAL AND LEADERSHIP GIFTS

Objectives

- Define the gifts of pastoring, administration, leadership and wisdom.
- Identify responsibilities that these gifts involve.
- Read examples of people with these gifts.

Main Ideas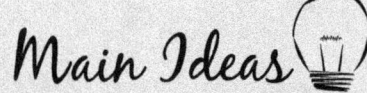

- Pastors are leaders, who in following the call of God and His people, lead the ministry of a local church.
- The pastor works in coordination with the other leaders of the church.

Introduction

How would a football team perform without a coach? Would a boat arrive at its destination with no one at the helm? How could an orchestra play in harmony without a conductor? Functions like these are those that God has delegated to the pastors, administrators, and leaders. Their ministries are essential for guiding the church in the accomplishment of its mission in this world (Ephesians 4:11).

The Gift of Pastoring

In this section we will learn about the gift of pastoring.

Pastor is the translation of the Greek word "poimen" which means the one who cares for and feeds the flock, and it is applied to someone who pastors a church (Ephesians 4:11). The pastor is a minister, called by God and the people, to run a local church.

There are also others who have the gift of serving as pastors of a group of Christians for a certain time period. In other words, they have received a special ability from God to care for other believers and guide them in their spiritual growth. Here are some examples: a cell group leader, a discipler, a children's pastor, a youth pastor, a women's or men's ministries leader and others.

Pastoral Responsibilities

The call to ministry as a pastor who leads a local church is distinguished by the passion to build, equip, and guide Christians in their spiritual growth and in the life of Christian service (Acts 18:24-26, Galatians 1:6-12, 2 Timothy 4:1-2). We can compare the pastor's ministry in leadership with the work of a sport's coach or the conductor of an orchestra. Their job is not to do all the work of the ministry, but to train believers so that they can serve. According to the New Testament, the quality of a pastor's work is measured by the quality of the ministries developed by the members of his or her church. It is for this function of leading the congregation that pastors also

Pastoral Gifts
Many ministries and functions are required to take care of a local church. One person is not able to do them all. For this reason, Christ gives gifts among all members of the church, so that each member of the body can minister to others, therefore serving in a pastoral role. The gifts identified in the Bible that have a pastoral significance are these:
Pastor / Teacher (spiritual feeding)
Prophecy (lead the flock)
Wisdom and knowledge (instruct, guide)
Faith (encourage, trust)
Exhortation (lifting, strengthening the fallen)
Mercy (restore, help)
Help and serve (the needy)
Management and leadership

need the gifts of administration and leadership. A pastor has the following responsibilities:

- Preaching and teaching the Word of God (1 Timothy 5:17, Titus 1:9).

- Directing the ministry of the church so that it can grow in all dimensions (John 10:3-4, 1 Peter 2:25 and 5:3).

- Restoring, correcting, encouraging, and consoling (Ezekiel 34:10).

- Protecting, looking after, serving, watching over (John 10:10-15).

- Improving and equipping (Ephesians 4:11-12).

John Wesley

John Wesley was born on June 17, 1703 in the home of an Anglican pastor in Epworth, England. In 1728, at age 23, he was ordained as an Anglican priest and two years later he received his Master of Arts. While at the University of Oxford, he presided over the "the Saint's Club" but in spite of this he did not have personal assurance that his sins had been forgiven. The faith and testimony of the Moravians impressed Wesley. On May 24, 1738, after attending a Moravian prayer meeting, he had a special experience: ".... I received the assurance that my sins had been forgiven."

Soon after, he realized that the experience he had received was heart sanctity and that this was different from and came after his conversion. The work of sanctification or Christian perfection became the key theme of his sermons and writings. God used his ministry to bring revival throughout England. John Wesley was the founder of the Methodist Church and the one who developed Wesleyan-Holiness theology.

During the 40 years of his ministry, he rode on horseback covering about 8,300 km. a year. He used this time to read and prepare sermons because sometimes he preached up to eight times a day. He was a man of great discipline; during his life, he wrote 40,000 sermons and 3,000 books and pamphlets on various topics such as theology, science, logic, medicine and music.

Burnis Bushong says that Wesley preached his last sermon at the age of 87, an event at which his friends had to help him stand in the pulpit. On March 2, 1791, he entered the presence of God. Before his death he said, "The best thing is that God is with us."

The Gift of Administration

In the next section we will study the gift of administration.

The gift of administration is the ability to organize well, develop plans and objectives for the short, medium and long term, and coordinate and direct church activities. Those with this gift have the desire and ability

---

Confirmation questions for the gift of being a pastor
- Do I clearly identify with the responsibilities of a pastor?
- Would I like to invest my life in giving spiritual guidance to families in different stages of their lives?
- Do I like helping people to achieve their Christian vocation?
- Do I feel love and compassion for people without a pastor?
- Do I feel responsible when someone is going through problems of sin or sorrow?

Duties of the church in support of pastors
1 Corinthians 9:14
1 Timothy 5:17-18
Hebrews 13:7 and 17
Philippians 2:29
1 Thessalonians 5:12-13
Romans 15:30.

Scriptures pertaining to the gift of administration
Exodus 18:13-27
I Corinthians 12:28

Lesson 2 - Pastoral and Leadership Gifts

Confirmation questions for the gift of administration
• Do I feel uncomfortable with clutter and disorganization?
• Do I identify clearly with the responsibilities of a manager?
• Do I like to keep things in order and anticipate likely problems?
• Do I like to plan the steps needed to achieve objectives?
• Do I feel comfortable delegating tasks to others?
• Do I work well under pressure?

to set goals according to the vision they have received from God; they communicate those goals to other people and motivate and lead them to achieve the objectives by designing, organizing and overseeing the process (1 Corinthians 12:28). Good leaders need administrators.

The task of administration is not only about the financial issues of the church, but also the aspects of institutional management, in coordination with the pastor and church leaders.

The Administrator's Responsibilities

The word "administration" comes from the Greek "kuberneseis" which means "one who pilots a ship," which refers to the person at the helm of a boat who helps it to reach its destination without problems. It can also be translated as "governor" or "the one who presides" and in this sense it is closely related to the gift of leadership. In the Bible there are two qualities required of those who serve as administrators:

- Faithfulness   1 Corinthians 4:2, Luke 16:10-12

- Diligence   Luke 14:28

Miguel Ángel Mejía Flores

Miguel Angel Mejia Flores was born on September 28, 1926 in El Salvador. In his youth he studied for just two years at high school, but served as an administrator in a private enterprise. He married Celia Sara Perez in 1949 and has been a member of the Church of the Nazarene since 1966. Miguel served as a Sunday School teacher, a leader on the local church board and on the district advisory board.

Parallel to his life in the church, he became the sales manager in the company where he worked, where he was known for his diligence and success in his work and for the enthusiasm with which he evangelized employees at the office for 23 years.

From 1974 to 1999, he was the administrator of the Nazarene Seminary of the Americas (SENDAS) in Costa Rica, (1974-1987 and 1992-1999). After, he became the administrator of the Church of the Nazarene Regional Office for the MAC Region (1987 - 1992).

During his service he made significant achievements, including the expansion and construction of new infrastructure for SENDAS and his work as music teacher and director of the seminary student's choir. His impeccable testimony is expressed by his own words: "Being a faithful Christian is the root of great triumph; surrender to the Lord and expect great things."

The Gift of Leadership

In this section, we will study the gift of leadership.

Scriptures pertaining to the gift of leadership:
*Exodus 18:13-27
Matthew 8:1-4, 20:27
Luke 14:28, 16:10-12
John 13:1-7
1 Corinthians 4:2-12:28
1 Timothy 6:1-2
2 Thessalonians 3:4*

The word leadership is translated from the Greek verb "proistemi" which means: to preside, lead and direct. These people motivate, inspire and organize others with spiritual authority for ministerial work (Romans 12:8, 1 Thessalonians 5:12). The style of spiritual leadership is in many ways opposed to the world, as the Christian leader must have a servant's attitude like Jesus (Matthew 20:27).

Most people have the potential to become leaders, even if they are unaware of it. This means that you have skills, abilities, qualities, and hidden talents that can be developed with training and practice. Spiritual leadership is a gift and a calling that has to do with the direction of the church in its mission.

Qualities of Spiritual Leader

The leader is the one who sets the pace in the church. When the leader does not have a plan to achieve his vision, he is just a dreamer. That's why the spiritual gift of leadership is accompanied by the gift of administration (Exodus 18:13-27). A good spiritual leader is distinguished by the following attributes:

- Vision. The leader has worthy goals that are hard to reach and require long-term investment of time and resources.

- A practical plan with medium-term goals.

- Willpower or healthy ambition to put the plan into action.

- The main fruit of his or her ministry is to develop leaders (2 Timothy 2:2, Ephesians 4:11-12).

Qualities of a spiritual leader
- Loyal (1 Timothy 6:1-2; 2 Thessalonians 3:4)
- Teachable (Titus 3:14; Job 6:24)
- Subject to authority (Romans 13:1-2; John 14:12)
- Obedient (Hebrews 13:17)
- Humble (Romans 12:3)
- Positive (Romans 8:28; Philippians 4:8,13)
- Servant's heart (Matthew 18:1-4)

Bruno and Liliana Radziszewski

Dr. Bruno Radziszewski (1946-2005) stood out as a pastor and leader of the Church of the Nazarene in the SAM Region, with his wife, Liliana, whom he married in 1986.

Both served as Evangelism Coordinators in Paraguay. Between 1988 and 1994, they served as Directors of Evangelism in Brazil, the Southern Cone and Ecuador. They also served as Area Directors for the Southern Cone.

In 1994, he was appointed Regional Director for South America, which included a move to Ecuador. The following year, for reasons of safety, the Regional Office was moved to Argentina. There, he served in the same position until June 21, 2005, when the Lord received him into His presence after Bruno suffered from heart problems.

Three styles or types of leaders by Roger L. Smalling:
- "Pioneers" are visionaries who open new fields of mission and are generally bad administrators.
- "Managers" are administrators who follow the pioneering leader and transmit their vision. They are able to find and organize resources to achieve the vision in an orderly and progressive fashion.
- "Caretakers" are the maintainers. They ensure the spiritual development of the people; they keep people happy and satisfied. But due to their lack of vision and goals, they do not see much growth.

Confirmation questions for the gift of leadership
• Do I have the ability to influence and motivate others to work on projects to meet the needs of the church?
• Do I easily let others follow me?
• Am I interested in sharing ministry responsibilities with others?
• Do I like to train others to serve the Lord?
• Do I feel it is my duty to take initiative and provide direction to organize others in the work?

During all those years, Bruno´s wife Liliana served beside him as his assistant and administrator at each function. Currently, Liliana lives in Pilar, Buenos Aires, with their daughters. She continues to serve full-time as a missionary of the Church of the Nazarene, as the legal representative of the Church in Argentina, as Regional Coordinator of Nazarene Missions International, and as Administrative Manager of the Regional Office (Mujer Valiosa TV: 2008).

The Gift of Wisdom

In this section we will study the gift of wisdom.

The gift of wisdom is characterized by the ability to discern the practical application of God's truths to special situations (1 Corinthians 12:8). In the Word, the source of all wisdom is God (Romans 11:33; 1 Corinthians 1:21) and His wisdom has been revealed to us in Christ (1 Corinthians 1:30) and through the Holy Spirit (1 Corinthians 2:7-10).

The gift of wisdom is closely related to the ministries of teaching and preaching, since it includes the special ability to apply knowledge in practical and particular situations that require solutions (1 Kings 3:5-28).

Responsibility of the Person with the Gift of Wisdom:

- Helping others to resolve difficult issues through counseling.
- Warning others against taking wrong courses of action (for example, in strategy or theology).
- Collaborating with leaders to develop plans and work projects.
- Working with teams to interpret and apply the Word to situations today.
- Providing guidance on the development of the church.
- Giving guidance concerning the best ways to utilize human resources and materials of the church.

Phineas F. Bresee

Phineas Franklin Bresee was born in Franklin (New York) in 1838 to a Christian family. He became a Christian at the age of 16 and from his youth had clarity about his call to pastoral ministry. At 28, he was filled with the Holy Spirit. After pastoring several Methodist churches in Iowa and California, many leaders appreciated this young man's many gifts, most notably the gift of wisdom. Bresee had a knack for organizing the work of the church so that it grew not only in number but also in finances.

By then he was named pastor in the Methodist University "Matthew Simpson" (Iowa) which was having serious economic problems. Bresee designed a plan to save the university from financial ruin and finally

Scriptures pertaining to the gift of wisdom
1 Kings 3:9 and 16-28
1 Corinthians 2:7-10;
4:1;12:8
Ephesians 3:3-6

succeeded in doing so after much effort and sacrifice. His gift of wisdom was linked to his passion for the poor which led him to become involved in the social problems of the community.

At age 45, he moved to be a pastor in California where he found many challenges. The population surrounding the church in Los Angeles was made up of immigrants from many different cultures. Bresee took advantage of these circumstances and the church grew rapidly.

Bresee also had a special wisdom for preaching and teaching holiness. From 1890, Bresee made the doctrine of holiness the ultimate goal of all his preaching, so he led holiness revival campaigns from California to Illinois. Bresee faced a lot of opposition because of his emphasis on holiness and his work with poor immigrants.

After several years and going through various ministerial functions in the Methodist Church, finally at the age of 58, Bresee and his friend Widney, decided to start a new holiness denomination with the congregation of Peniel Mission. Bresee and Widney were the first leaders of the Church of the Nazarene. The church grew from 300 to 1500 people in eight years with a number of sister churches (including a congregation of Mexican and Japanese immigrant workers) in different places in California as well as out of the state.

Bresee continued as pastor, university president, and as General Superintendent of the Church of the Nazarene until his death in 1915, at the age of 77. The gift of wisdom that the Holy Spirit gave Bresee, together with gifts for pastoring, leading, teaching, administrating and living compassionately, among others, led him to be the Lord's instrument in the founding of the Church of the Nazarene which today has become the largest holiness denomination around the world.

Confirmation questions for the gift of wisdom
• Do I have the ability to solve practical problems in the church?
• Do I like helping people make good decisions?
• Do people ask for my advice on various issues?
• Am I happy to help leaders to find the best strategies for the church mission?
• Do I have the ability to teach others to apply the principles of the Word when they make decisions in their daily lives?

What Did We Learn?

The gifts of pastoral service, administration, leadership, and wisdom are essential to enable the church to function well. Good leaders and pastors surround themselves with good administrators and Christians with the gift of wisdom so that together they can lead the church to grow in a healthy way.

Lesson 2 - Pastoral and Leadership Gifts

Activities

Time 20'

INSTRUCTIONS:

1. As discussed in this lesson, the gifts of pastoring, administration, wisdom and leadership are essential for the proper functioning of the church. Write a definition of each of these gifts in your own words.
___
___
___

2. What are the required qualities for a pastor according to 1 Timothy 3:1-7?
___
___
___

3. How could you identify the people in your church who have these gifts?
___
___
___

4. Consider the work of your pastor and think of some ways you could support him or her. Then write a list of these items and this week talk to your pastor about it.
___
___
___

5. The leader's game.

A student leaves the room, so he/she does not hear or see the group planning. The remaining students are placed in a circle and a volunteer will act as the leader. The leader will discreetly direct the others with movements that everyone will follow, taking care not to reveal the identity of the leader. Once the action is agreed upon, the student is brought back in and is instructed to observe the behavior of his/her peers, trying to identify the leader in only 3 minutes.

After finishing this exercise, share ideas on what you have learned about leadership through this dynamic.
___
___
___

Lesson 3

Teaching and Preaching Gifts

Objectives
- Define the gifts of education, knowledge, discernment and prophecy.
- Identify the responsibilities that go along with these gifts.
- Read examples of people with these gifts.

Main Ideas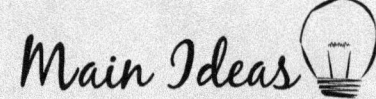
- Teachers and preachers develop essential ministries for the growth of the church.
- The gifts of teaching and knowledge are complementary.

Introduction

Have you ever wondered how teaching, wisdom, knowledge and prophecy are related? Do you think only "scholars" can be teachers in the church? Do you think that prophets speak for God? In this lesson we will study these gifts to answer these questions.

The Gift of Teaching

In this section we will study about the gift of teaching.

Scriptures pertaining to the gift of teaching
Acts 13:1; 1 Corinthians 12:28; Ephesians 4:11; James 3; Titus 1:9

The gift of teaching ("didasko" in the Greek language) in the Bible does not only refer to transmitting information but rather to the communication of spiritual truths that people need to grow into the image of Christ. The gift of teaching is also the special ability to study the Word of God in order to build up the church. Since all Christians are disciples that never stop growing into Christlikeness, the church needs brothers and sisters with the gift of teaching. In the Bible this gift appears joined together grammatically with the pastor who leads a local congregation. But not only pastors receive this gift.

Responsibilities of Teachers

- In depth study of Scripture.
- Understanding the questions and needs of their students.
- Putting the profound truths into words that everyone can understand.
- Knowing and using teaching methods to transfer knowledge in an interesting, varied and entertaining way.
- Being a living example of the life of holiness (Titus 1:9).

Jesus of Nazareth

Jesus is the best example of the gift of teaching. He shows us that a teacher's words reach only as far as the example of the holy life demonstrated

Confirmation questions pertaining to the gift of teaching
• Do I know already or would I like to specialize in teaching techniques?
• Am I interested in researching some Bible passages beyond what they teach at church?
• Am I creative enough to explain or illustrate complex topics in simple terms?
• Do I organize my ideas to present them to others?
• Do I like to work hard so others can understand and put into practice the Word of God in their lives?

by the teacher (John 14:6). And Jesus lived one hundred percent what he taught. S. Gordon said: "Jesus was what he said even before he acted; He lived it before teaching it; and he lived it beyond what he could teach" (Price). His life example gave Him authority to teach and it inspired confidence in His audience, two very important aspects for education so that the teaching does not fall on deaf ears.

The Lord believed that teaching was a powerful tool to transform lives and shape ideals, attitudes and behavior. Jesus understood human nature (John 2:25) and it was this knowledge that enabled Him to identify the needs of his listeners. Jesus had an intimate and personal knowledge of the heavenly Father and of the Scriptures. He knew that teachers nurture students from their abundance, not from their emptiness.

Jesus taught individuals, groups and crowds. He taught people of different races, ages, sexes, religions, occupations and social statuses. In each case, He used a variety of teaching methods and used available resources. He used all the methodologies that are used today: questions, stories, conversations, discussions, plays, objects, projects and demonstrations. His method is still used today by good teachers: His introductions were direct, and His illustrations and applications were appropriate for the needs and questions of his listeners.

As J. M. Price said: "No one had better training for his work as a teacher than Jesus." Jesus was first and foremost the Master teacher; He never stopped teaching (Price).

General indicators that one may have the gift of teaching:
- He or she is committed to the truth, the relevance and the authority of the Bible.
- He or she has the responsibility to study and prepare for the task of teaching.
- He or she emphasizes details that lead to a correct interpretation of the Scripture.
- He or she has the ability to explain and apply Biblical truths that contribute to the growth of the Body of Christ.
- He or she has the willingness and ability to support and teach the truth while facing opposition.

The Gift of Knowledge

In this section we will define the gift of knowledge.

The gift of knowledge (from the Greek "ginosko") refers not to intellectual knowledge, but to the ability that comes from God to study, investigate, collect information, analyze data, learn and be able to rapidly put the information into practice so it can be shared to benefit the church. Knowledge is not opposed to faith; on the contrary, knowledge and faith are related and together provide a firm foundation. This gift is closely related to the gift of teaching, preaching and writing.

Responsibilities of the person with the gift of knowledge

- Since this gift can lead to pride, it is important to stay humble.
- Prioritizing: focusing study and research on matters that are helpful for the progress and edification of the church.
- Striving to communicate the conclusions to the church in a clear and simple way.

The gift of knowledge can be applied in several ways in ministry such as in writing books, researching an area of theology, ministerial practices or church growth, and studying the needs of the community where the church ministers to find trends.

Confirmation questions for the gift of knowledge
• Do I like investigating a case to get to the bottom of the truth?
• Do I have the patience and dedication to study a problem to find the best answer?
• If I am in a group of people trying to solve a problem am I one of the first to propose a plan to find the best solution?
• Do I like that people come to me for answers?

Scriptures pertaining to the gift of knowledge
1 Corinthians 2:12-13
Ephesians 1:17-19

- Being careful to avoid belittling people who do not have the same level of knowledge.

- Leading professionals and scholars to know Jesus Christ as Savior, using their area of specialty as a tool.

Martin Luther

Martin Luther was born in Eisleben, Germany in 1483 and died in Thuringia in 1546. Contrary to the wishes of his parents, Martin became an Augustinian monk in 1505 and began studying theology at the University of Wittenberg, where he received his doctorate in 1512.

As a professor, he began to question some practices of the Roman Catholic Church. After spending years researching the Bible, he defended the doctrines of the universal priesthood of believers and salvation by faith, which are both pillars of the Protestant Reformation. Luther's criticism reflected a fairly widespread climate of discontent because of the corruption into which the leaders of the Church had fallen. Luther's protest escalated until 1517 when he decided to make public his writings. He nailed his 95 Thesis to the door of Wittenberg Castle.

The priesthood of all believers implies the Christian's personal and direct relationship with God. This divided the church leaders, who declared themselves as the only mediators between God and the congregation and the only ones who could access and interpret the Bible for the people. Luther also defended the right of every believer to read the Bible freely. But for people to read the Bible, it needed to be translated from the original languages (Greek and Latin) to the languages of the people. Luther himself translated the Bible into German providing a version used by many people during the centuries. Martin Luther is remembered as one of the great reformers of the Christian Church (Woodbridge, 1998).

The Gift of Prophecy

In this section we will study the gift of prophecy.

Scriptures pertaining to the gift of prophecy
Deuteronomy 13:1-6
Deuteronomy 18-22
Acts 13:1; 21:10-11
1 Corinthians 14:29-38

The word prophet (in Greek "prophetes") at the time of the early church often meant teaching the Word of God. The task of the prophet was primarily to build up, comfort and encourage the believers (1 Timoteo 4:13-14 and Acts 13). The prophet's words did not have equal authority with Scripture and if contradicted, the prophet was considered false and his message was rejected by the church (1 Thessalonians 5:9-21). As for the unbelievers, the prophet's message was meant to make them aware of their sin.

As for the resemblance to the prophetic ministry of the Old Testament, in 1 Corinthians 13:8-9 the apostle Paul explains that the ministry of prophecy, the direct revelation of God's mind, was completed in Christ. This is because in Christ, God revealed His will to all human beings and His will is accessible to us in His Word (see also 2 Peter 1:19).

In conclusion, we describe the gift of prophecy as a special ability from the Holy Spirit to communicate and reveal God's will in His Word to people. This is the role of preachers and teachers today.

The Responsibilities of the Christian with the Gift of Prophecy

- Studying deeply the Word of God.
- Keeping informed about different aspects of today's world.
- Encouraging, strengthening and comforting the brethren (Acts 15:32, 1 Corinthians 14:3).
- Reflecting on contemporary events in light of the Word.
- Knowing and using public speaking methods.

Charles H. Spurgeon

Charles H. Spurgeon was born in 1834 in Kelveden, England. His grandfather and father were pastors and coal miners. As a child, his mother had instilled in him a desire for the study of the Word.

As a teenager, he rebelled against God and it was not until he was 16 years old that he accepted Christ as Lord and Savior. His first ministries were teaching children, handing out tracts and visiting the poor. Early in the morning he studied the Bible and prayed. At night after attending school, he taught the Word. At age 16 he joined an organization of lay preachers and was soon dubbed the "boy preacher." He preached in chapels, outdoors, in villages and in homes.

At 18 years of age (1852), he became a pastor at Waterbeach, located near Cambridge. His chapel was an old barn. The first Sunday twelve people attended, but the church was growing, thanks to his hard work. The following year, to his surprise, he was invited to preach in the church of New Park Street, a leading Baptist church in London, whose membership was 232 people. They had gone months without a pastor. This church had lost members consistently, and the first Sunday he preached 80 people attended. The membership started to grow and they continued inviting him until, in 1854, he was asked to accept the position of pastor.

Every Sunday the church was completely full and the people who did not come in heard the preaching from the streets. The building was expanded again and again, but there was never enough space, so they rented other buildings. At age 23, he preached in the largest available auditorium holding 23,654 people. By the end of 1891, after 37 years of ministry, he had baptized 14,460 people and had a church membership of 5,311.

Spurgeon published one sermon per week beginning in 1855. He also founded a seminary for pastors and established the Stockwell Orphanage,

The Gift of Prophecy
The ministry of the prophets was developed in Old Testament times. Their ministry consisted of the "proclamation of the divine purposes of salvation and glory to be available in the future through the coming of the Messiah. " The Apostle Peter says in 2 Peter 2:1 that in the early church, Christian teachers played a role in ministry similar to the ancient prophets. The difference is that the teachers based their principles on the written word and the prophet based their principles on the word that God personally spoke to them (Vine 2007).

Confirmation questions for the gift of prophecy
• Do I have the discipline to study the Word?
• Do I like to learn about the social, political and economic realities, etc?
• Do I feel responsible for teaching Biblical principles so others can make right choices in everyday affairs?
• When I speak, do people pay attention?
• Do I like to analyze the preaching of others?

Scriptures pertaining to the gift of discernment
1 Corinthians 12:10
2 Corinthians 11:14-15
Acts 8:26; 10:3; 12:7-10; 16:16-18; 27:23-24
2 Pedro 2:1; 2 Corinthians 11:14-15
2 Thessalonians 2:9
Revelations 16:14

which housed 500 children, divided into family groups, living in married couples' homes.

Charles Spurgeon died on January 31, 1892 at 56 years of age after 40 years of ministry. He preached over 3,500 sermons (Jay, 1984).

The Gift of Discernment

In this section we will learn about the gift of discernment.

The gift of discernment is a supernatural ability that comes from God to distinguish between God given manifestations and those with human or diabolical origins.

The gift of discernment is very necessary for leaders in contexts where many voices are raised, all who pretend to speak for God. They confuse people and divert the truth. Satan, the enemy of the Church, attempts to destroy the Church and divert it from holiness and its mission through deception (Acts 13:6-12). Sometimes Satan uses people who teach false doctrines (1 Timothy 4:1).

This gift is also required to free those who are afflicted, oppressed and tormented by Satan (Acts 16:16). Christians with the gift of discernment are those who pray for the demon possessed to be freed.

Responsibilities of a Christian with the Gift of Discernment

- Living a holy life. This ministry is not for the faint of spirit or immature believers.

- Avoiding making hasty judgments: it is necessary to test the spirits (1 John 4:1).

- Using Biblical criteria to test the spirits (1 John 4:2,3; James 3:14-17; Corinthians 12:3).

- Avoiding extremes (for instance, seeing demons in all people with problems).

- Teaching people to take responsibility for their actions rather than blaming demons for the irresponsible behavior.

- Not making a show of ministry; protecting the reputation of the church and the people involved.

- Knowing how to evangelize and disciple a person who has been freed.

- Knowing what ways Satan uses in a particular context to enslave people.

- Praying and fasting is required with this ministry.

Peter and Paul

Several of the apostles had the gift of discernment. Peter, for example, noted the hypocrisy of Ananias and Sapphira who lied to the church by stating they had brought as an offering all the money from the sale of a property. When Peter discovered this, they both dropped dead in front of the congregation (Acts 5:1-11).

On another occasion, Peter discovered Simon the magician's bad intentions, when he offered the apostles money in order to "buy" the power they had from the Holy Spirit to heal the sick (Acts 8:18-25).

Paul also had this gift, which he used to detect the malicious intentions of Elymas or Bar-Jesus, a Jewish magician and false prophet from Cyprus who gave counsel to the Proconsul (government official) of the island. The Proconsul showed interest but Elymas argued with Paul so much that it became difficult for the Proconsul to accept the gospel message (Acts 13:10). The Proconsul believed Paul's message after Paul rebuked the magician who then became blind. Another time when Paul was in Philippi, he met a girl who was being exploited by others who profited from a "divination spirit" that had possessed her. She ran after Paul and his companions for days shouting that they were servants of the Most High God. Finally Paul commanded the spirit in the name of Jesus Christ to leave her, and she was released. The men who exploited her reported the incident, and Paul and Silas were imprisoned until they were miraculously released (Acts 16:11-40).

How can I know if I have the gift of discernment?

- I feel compassion for people who are slaves of evil.

- It's easier for me than others to tell when something is not from God.

- Sometimes I can recognize a spiritual phony (hypocrite).

- People ask me for advice to distinguish right from wrong.

These statements may be indications that you have the gift of discernment.

What Did We Learn?

The gifts of teaching, wisdom, knowledge and prophecy are fundamental to guiding Christians in their holistic growth.

Several of these gifts may come together and are complementary. For example, the gift of prophecy relates to the ability to skillfully preach the Word of God and apply it to everyday living.

Lesson 3 - Teaching and Preaching Gifts

Activities

Time 20'

INSTRUCTIONS:

1. Mention some of the qualities of a Christian teacher who has been a positive influence in your life.
   _____
   _____
   _____

2. 1 Corinthians 12:8 mentions the gift of knowledge. Give examples of how you can use this gift in the church.
   _____
   _____
   _____

3. What are the dangers of the gift of prophecy, such as the ability to predict events? What warning does Jesus give to his disciples concerning this in Matthew 7:15-23; 24:11 and chapters 23-24?
   _____
   _____
   _____

4. List three examples where it is required to apply the gift of wisdom.
   _____
   _____
   _____

5. Divide students into two groups. One group gathers those who believe they have the gifts of teaching and knowledge. Its members will write a list of tips or recommendations for preachers and those who have the gift of discernment.

In the other group, gather those that that have gifts of prophecy and discernment. Their task is to write a list of tips or recommendations for Christian teachers. After three minutes, each group presents to the others their advice.

Lesson 4

Evangelism and Spiritual Counseling Gifts

Objectives

- Define the gifts of evangelism, faith, miracles, healing, intercession and exhortation (spiritual counseling).
- Identify the responsibilities that these gifts require.

Main Ideas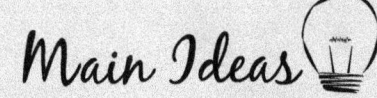

- The gift of exhortation is aimed at equipping spiritual counselors so that they can encourage, comfort and admonish others.
- The gifts of evangelism, faith, miracles, healing and intercession are essential to win others to Christ.

Introduction

Evangelism, faith, intercessory prayer and miracles are gifts related to the ministry of winning others to Christ. Some of these gifts have to do with the skill and passion of sharing the message of salvation with others, while others relate to miraculous signs that lead many unbelievers to believe and give their lives to Jesus Christ. Also, we will study the gift of exhortation, which in today's church, is related to the ministry of spiritual counseling.

Scriptures pertaining to the gift of evangelism
Acts 14:13-21
Romans 10:14-15
Ephesians 4:11

The Gift of Evangelism

In this section we will study the gift of evangelism.

Although all the disciples of Jesus have the responsibility to share their testimony with others, some Christians receive a passion and ability from the Holy Spirit to lead others to reconciliation with God. This gift is distinguished by a sense of urgency to communicate the gospel to all the people that they can. For these people, once they have received some training, evangelizing and discipling others becomes as normal as breathing. It has been estimated that at least ten percent of committed Christians have this gift.

Responsibilities of the Evangelist:

- Allowing the Spirit to show you who to testify to (Acts 8:5-6, 26-40).
- Being open to talking to all kinds of people.
- Not feeling spiritually superior to other Christians.
- Learning to present the plan of salvation and leading others to conversion.
- Living life with a holiness testimony that others can emulate.
- Teaming up with pastors and church disciplers.

Confirmation questions for the gift of evangelism
- Do I feel a great burden to pray (more than other Christians) for the lost?
- Am I sad for individuals and families who suffer because of their sinful habits?
- When someone accepts Christ as Savior, is it one of the happiest moments of my life?
- Do I feel compelled at all times and everywhere to start conversation with strangers to bear witness to what Christ has done in me?
- Do I like to present the message of salvation in simple, creative and contemporary language?

- Training others who have the same gift.
- Praying for unbelievers, that the Spirit would prepare their hearts.

Bill Bright

Bill Bright (1921-2003) was born in Oklahoma, United States. He was a businessman until his conversion in 1944 at the First Presbyterian Church of Hollywood, California. Soon after, he began his Biblical studies. It was in Fuller Seminary that he felt a personal call from God to help fulfill the Great Commission (Matthew 28:19). From that time on, he began to evangelize with Campus Crusade for Christ which he led with his wife, Vonette. Currently this movement involves 27,000 full-time workers and more than 225,000 volunteers in 190 countries.

On one occasion, on a plane before the flight departure, he led to Christ the person who was sitting on his left. Then, during the flight, he evangelized the person in the seat to his right. Bill had a special gift for bringing people to give their lives to Jesus and accept Him as their Lord and Savior.

Bill received several doctorates and the Templeton Prize, which is awarded to individuals who have contributed to the advance of the gospel. He wrote over 100 books including the widespread method of evangelization, "Four Spiritual Laws," and in 1956 he produced the JESUS Film.

Scriptures pertaining to the gift of faith
Joshua 10:12-14
Matthew 8:5-13, 17:20; 21:18-22
Mark 4:37-40
John 11:41-44
Romans 4:18-21
1 Corinthians 12:9
James 1:5-8
Hebrews 11:1-40

The Gift of Faith

In this section we will study the gift of faith.

The gift of faith is the ability to place trust in Almighty God to meet real needs in miraculous ways with a firm assurance the needs will be met. It is not an irrational faith, but one that is based on His promises, in the knowledge of His love, and belief that as individuals and as a church we are serving according to His plan and according to His will (Matthew 17:20). Christians with the gift of faith have the ability to encourage others to trust and wait for divine provision in a given situation.

Responsibilities of a Christian with the gift of faith:

- Taking time to listen and encourage others.
- Praying for others in need.
- Encouraging church leaders as they pass through discouragement.
- Being careful not to confuse faith with personal dreams (this is especially important for those with the gift of leadership).
- Being aware that not everyone has this gift.

Confirmation questions for the gift of faith
• Am I naturally a person who motivates others?
• When others are discouraged around me, do I still have confidence that God is in control of the situation and He will show us the way out?
• Do I enjoy encouraging other Christians when they are in need?
• When I pray, do I generally think that God will work in response?
• Do I have no fear of asking God for "difficult" things because I'm sure there is nothing too difficult for God?

Lesson 4 - Evangelism and Spiritual Counseling Gifts

- Learning how to teach others to develop their faith.

Loida Morejon

Loida Morejon is a Nazarene leader in the Caribbean. On one occasion, when her father Andres Morejon was the district superintendent, an event occurred where Loida showed this gift of faith. During the celebration of the district assembly, hundreds of Nazarene brothers and sisters all from the island had arrived at the seminary facilities. Loida was responsible for providing lunch to everyone.

When it was time for lunch, seeing that the crowd of people in line had exceeded all expectations, her worried father went to the kitchen and asked her, "My child, what are we going to do? It is evident that the food will not be enough for all." Looking at her father firmly, Loida said, "Dad, the same Jesus who multiplied the loaves and the fishes is here today, and he'll multiply this meal." Loida and her assistants served the food with love as the line moved along. One by one each person received a plate and even the cooks and leaders ate their fill. Loida testifies, "God multiplied the food that day, but when we finished serving the last dish, there was nothing left to scrape out of the pot!"

Scriptures pertaining to the gift of miracles
Mark 2:1-12
Acts 3:1-8; 14:8-10
James 5:4-16
Exodus 14:21-31
Acts 12
2 Kings 4:1-7
John 2:1-11
Luke 9:16-17
Romans 15:17-20

The Gift of Miraculous Acts and Healing

In this section we will learn about the gifts of miraculous acts and healing.

Miracles are events in which God intervenes in times of crisis where our resources are depleted. A miracle is an act that cannot be generally explained by natural laws, but that happens at the right time and in response to the prayer of Christians. Miracles happen to testify to the love and care that God has for humans. The gift of healing is the desire and ability to minister health to people's lives whether spiritual, emotional or physical. Healing sometimes happens in an instant, in other times gradually and often as a result of care and treatment provided to the patient.

Responsibilities of the Christian with the gift of miraculous acts and healing:

- Engaging in worship with emphasis on prayer for the sick.
- Engaging in prayer vigils for the needs of the congregation or community.
- Keeping a notebook with people's prayer needs.
- Visiting, encouraging, and praying for the sick at their homes or in hospitals.
- In every case, giving the glory to God for the miracle and healing.

Confirmation questions for the gifts of miracles and healings
• Do I feel compassion for the sick?
• Do I have confidence in the supernatural power of God?
• Do I feel comfortable visiting, comforting and praying for the sick?
• Are there times that miracles and healings have occurred in response to my prayers?
• Is one of the greatest joys of my life when someone is healed or a miracle occurs in response to my prayer?

- Teaching others about this ministry.

Rosalino Santiago Pineda

A few years ago, Rosalino Santiago Pineda was a lay pastor in the Church of the Nazarene in Juchitan, Oaxaca. One of his daughters, Noemi, tells the following story:

Rosalino is a person of faith who prays for the sick and God heals them. His local church has grown partly due to the testimonies of healings. He has had a beautiful influence of faith on the lives of his grandchildren. They have learned to trust God for all their ailments, seeing the example of their grandfather. On countless occasions, when they were sick as children, they would pray with faith for healing and also they would pray when their pets were sick.

On one occasion, a car accidentally hit the children's dog named Lupo. When the children returned from school, they saw him injured and unable to walk. They cried and were very sad. Then, without saying a word, they knelt on the ground and prayed with great faith for their pet. To the surprise of the family and the adults present, their dog recovered and began to walk. It was an incredible healing.

This is a simple example of how children learn to pray with faith to God for healing. These children practice it whenever they have an opportunity to pray for others and healing happens.

Scriptures pertaining to the gift of healing
Mark 1:29-31
Mark 3:1-5
Acts 5:12-16, 8:6-7
Acts 14:8-15

The Gift of Intercessory Prayer

In this section we will study about passionate prayer for the needs of others.

While praying for others is the responsibility of all Christians, some believers have the gift of intercession, which is evident by the desire and discipline to devote time to pray for the needs of others, beyond what Christians usually do.

Responsibilities of an intercessor:

- Identifying the person to pray for and being immersed in their needs and sufferings (2 Corinthians 5:21).

- Intercession for others involves pleading, like a lawyer who pleads for the lives of others (Hebrews 7:25).

- Feeling deeply the pain of the Lord for these suffering people.

- Giving up pleasures and physical comforts to make time for prayer and fasting.

- Praying for the unsaved with a list of names.

Confirmation questions for the gift of intercessory prayer
• Do I feel motivated to find time alone to pray for others?
• Is it natural for me to put the needs of others before my own when I pray?
• Am I happy to be part of what God is doing in other places through my prayer life?
• Do people ask me to pray for their needs?
• Do I have no problem praying for a need for several months before receiving the answer?
• Do I want to identify with those who suffer, depriving myself from some comfort for a time, so I can better pray for them?

- Reaching out to those who are suffering in the church and community.
- Finding out about the needs of missionaries around the world.

Rees Howells

Rees Howells was born in Wales in 1879 and lived during the Second World War. Rees started praying intensely for months for a single person, until he received God's reply. Then he began to intercede for the nations of the world and for missionaries.

Howells learned to be guided by the voice of the Holy Spirit who showed him who he should pray for. Rees thought it was essential that while he prayed he should identify himself with that person. Once he spent four months praying for underprivileged children in India and did not eat bread, tea, or sugar. He only ate a plate of stew every two days and slept on the floor. He prayed all day starting at five o'clock in the morning. On another occasion he isolated himself for ten months and prayed about starting a seminary in Swansea, South Wales. He prayed from six in the morning until five in the afternoon and ate once a day.

Howells said about this ministry: "God is looking for intercessors, but He rarely finds them. This expression of sorrow can be seen in the exclamation made by Isaiah 59:16 and Ezekiel 22:30... Perhaps some believers describe intercession as a form of intense prayer. And it is. There is a lot of emphasis placed on the word 'intense' because there are three elements of intercession that are not in the ordinary prayer: identification, agony and authority" (Boyer, 1983).

Scriptures pertaining to the gift of intercessory prayer
Daniel 6:11-12; 9:1-4
Luke 11:1-13
Colossians 4:12-13
1 Timothy 2: 1-4
James 5:15-18
Hebrews 8:1

The Gift of Exhortation or Spiritual Counseling

In this section we will study the gift of exhortation.

The word that is translated from the Greek for exhortation is parakaleo, which means to beg, insist, encourage, inspire courage, ask, comfort, console. The gift of exhortation is the ability the Holy Spirit gives to some of His children to encourage, admonish, give advice, and comfort others or persuade people to do or not to do something.

Responsibilities of people with the gift of exhortation:

- Encouraging those who are spiritually weak (Hebrews 3:13).
- Visiting and encouraging those who are absent from church services or activites (Hebrews 10:24-25).
- Encouraging those who doubt their commitment to Christ (1 Thessalonians 2:11-12).

Scriptures pertaining to the gift of exhortation
John 4:1-42
Acts 14: 21-22
Romans 12:6-8
2 Corinthians 1:3-7
1 Thessalonians 2:11; 5:14
1 Timothy 5:1

- Comforting those who are sad and admonishing with love and gentleness.

- Advising about how to deal with difficult family problems or interpersonal relationship problems in the church.

- Providing guidance based on Biblical principles.

- Always trusting in the Holy Spirit's guidance throughout the process.

James Clayton Dobson

Dr. James C. Dobson was born in Louisiana, USA in 1936 and is a member of the Church of the Nazarene. From an early age "Jim" joined his parents in their journey throughout the country preaching the gospel. He gave his life to Jesus at 3 years of age after his father preached. He got married in 1960 and has two children, Danae and Ryan.

From a young age he knew that his calling and passion were to help families to live by Biblical principles, so he decided to become a Christian counselor. He studied psychology at Point Loma Nazarene University, and obtained a Ph.D. in Child Development at the University of Southern California in 1967. In 1977 he founded the organization Focus on the Family. This ministry has a radio program that airs in over a dozen languages, in more than 7,000 radio stations, reaching 220 million people in a total of 164 countries.

Dobson is a writer and lecturer. He has worked on many government committees speaking for the family, "traditional" marriage (male-female) values, the rights of women, motherhood and children, among others. He has received numerous awards and recognitions. The Christianity Today magazine recently named him "America's most influential evangelical leader."

Confirmation questions for the gift of exhortation
• Have I been thanked for my words of encouragement and motivation?
• Do I find it natural to encourage and motivate others?
• Do people seek me out to tell me of their problems?
• Do I feel sorrow for the misery of my brothers and sisters and want to do something about it?
• Am I unafraid to confront someone when it is necessary?
• Do I have the ability to intercede when there is conflict between two or more people?

WHAT DID WE LEARN?

In this lesson we studied the importance of the gifts of evangelism, faith, miracles, healing, intercessory prayer and exhortation.

These gifts are essential if the church is to make an impact in the world and lead sinners to salvation. The gift of exhortation is essential for those that serve as spiritual advisors.

Lesson 4 - Evangelism and Spiritual Counseling Gifts

Activities

Time 20'

INSTRUCTIONS:

In the following activity, all students can work together to solve a problem that could occur in a local church.

1. The Situation:

Our church is planning to make an impact in the community through various evangelistic activities during Holy Week (the week before Easter Sunday). People with the gifts and ministries of evangelism, faith, miracles, healing, intercessory prayer and encouragement need to be organized in groups, so as to cover all the areas required for responsible evangelism, spiritual care and the incorporation of new believers in discipleship groups.

2. The design for this plan:

a) The plan must include all the gifts studied in this lesson.

b) For 5 minutes, the whole class will work to identify three to five general goals for these evangelistic activities. For example:

1. Visit 100 households in the community, making information cards with the information of those living in each house including their prayer requests.
2. Pray for 20 days for these people and their needs.
3. Visit each family again after 20 days to see how they are doing, to see if there has been a response to the prayer need, and to invite them to a special activity.
4. After the activity, follow up with the new disciples.
5. Follow up with others who have expressed interest.

c) For the next 5 minutes, the students are divided into work groups according to their gifts. Each group will make a list of their responsibilities and the tasks they will need to do to achieve these objectives.

d) Finally, each group will report on what they have accomplished with the rest of the class. Each group will choose a presenter who will have 1 minute to speak.

Lesson 5

Gifts of Compassion and Service

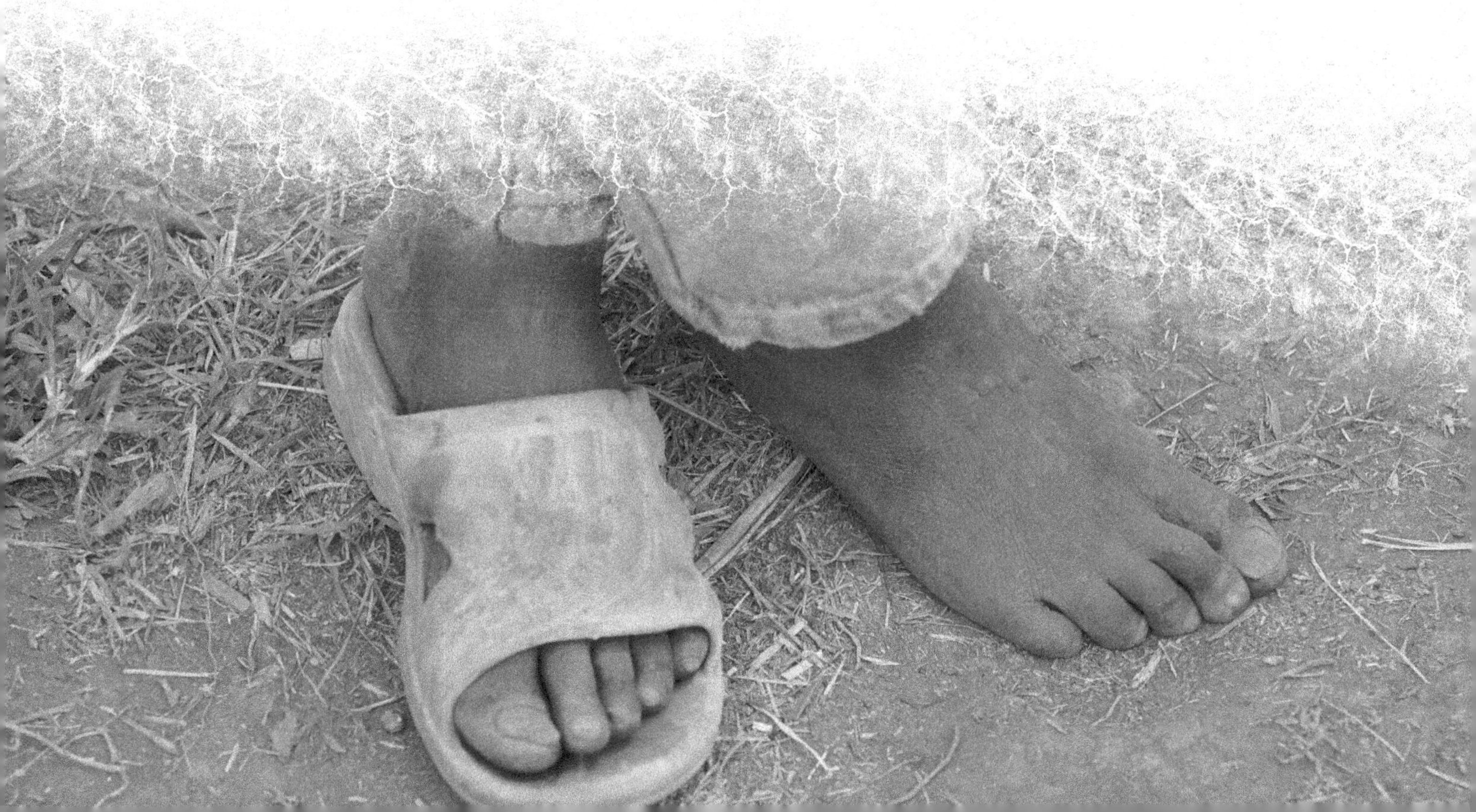

Objectives

- Define the gifts of compassion, help, hospitality, service and generosity.
- Identify the responsibilities that these gifts involve.

Main Ideas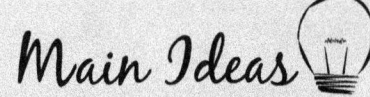

- The gifts of compassion and service help the church fulfill its social responsibility.
- These gifts were essential in the ministry of Jesus and the Early Church.
- Those with these gifts serve others according to their needs.

Introduction

Throughout the Bible, a Christian's responsibility to care for the suffering, for foreigners and the needy is obvious. Service to others as volunteers is one of the qualities of a healthy church that reflects the compassion of their Lord to the world. However, as discussed in this lesson, God places in the heart of some of His children a unique passion for helping those who are in need by giving gifts of compassion, service, support, hospitality and generosity.

The Gift of Compassion

In this section we will study the gift of compassion.

The gift of compassion can be seen in the desire and sensitivity to assist others, especially those who are facing crises or difficulties that they cannot resolve by themselves. People with this gift are actively involved in comforting, consoling and helping these people to regain their joy (Matthew 15:32, 18:33).

Scriptures pertaining to the gift of compassion
Matthew 25:37-40
Luke 10:25-37
Acts 9:36-42
Romans 12:4-8
James 1:27, 2:14-17

Responsibilities of the person with the gift of compassion:

- Responding to perceived needs that believers and the community may have.

- Participating in work teams to assist in disasters or natural catastrophes.

- Giving to the Church of the Nazarene's fund for hunger relief and disaster relief in the world.

- Being actively involved in Nazarene Compassionate Ministries.

- Encouraging others to contribute their time, money and talents in compassionate projects in the local church.

- Teaching people in the church and the community how to improve hygiene, nutrition, safety, etc.

School of Leadership - Discovering My Vocation in Christ

- Identifying community needs and organizing a neighborhood work plan to meet them.

Judy Marisol de Arenas

Judy Marisol de Arenas was born in 1965 in Panama and became a Christian as a teenager. While she was studying to be a pastor at the Nazarene Seminary of the Americas in Costa Rica, she received the vision from God of planting a church in the poorest place in Panama as part of her ministerial practice.

So in 2002, she began a mission in "El Vertedero" (the trash dump), located on the outskirts of the city of Chorrera. Large trucks arrive here to unload Panama City's garbage. It is not pleasant to breathe the air there, and there are many flies, rats, and vultures all around.

Marisol found families there living off what they could find in the mountains of waste: it is from this trash that they would find their food for the day. They lived in precarious homes built with materials from the dump, and tried to make a living by selling bits and pieces of rubbish. Their life was not easy, and they hardly had enough to eat each day. The children had no education and everyone was always exposed to diseases.

Marisol, with the help of other members of the church, took advantage of various resources to help and evangelize these families. The Evangecube, the JESUS Film, food supplies, lectures on nutrition and health, among others resources were used. Soon there were about 70 people attending church activities.

In a few years Marisol petitioned the government to help to build new homes and relocate these families to Playa Chiquita. Now they have a school for their children, clean water, electricity and also a Nazarene Church called "Luz de Esperanza" (Light of Hope) where 100 people gather to worship God.

Confirmation questions for the gift of compassion
- When I see someone in need, do I have the desire to do something to help?
- Do I enjoy spending my time helping others?
- Do I like to get involved in the ministry of compassion in my church?
- Do I have the ability to identify resources where others see none?
- Do I have the ability to help others manage available resources?
- Am I comfortable asking for contributions to assist in the needs of others?

Gifts of Service and Support

In this section we will learn about the gifts of service and support.

The gifts of service and support are similar. One focuses on people's needs, either of people or institutions, and the other supports leaders that serve in any ministry. They are distinguished by the desire and ability to identify the needs around them and meet them.

People with these gifts have a permanent attitude of service and wish to invest their time and talents in solving needs in the church and community. In all ministries, people with these gifts are needed. These people receive from God a special ability to use the available resources and provide a solution for the needs (Acts 6:1).

Examples of service ministries are varied: working with the elderly, orphans, widows, single mothers, providing child care for working mothers, among others.

Scriptures pertaining to the gifts of service and support
Luke 10:38-42
Luke 22:24-27
Mathew 25:35
1 Peter 4:9-10
Hebrews 13:1-2

Lesson 5 - Gifts of Compassion and Service

Examples of the gift of support include these: cooking, transporting, hospitality, cleaning, maintenance, hosting, among others.

Responsibility of Christians with the gift of service and support:

- Serving with love without complaining about the service provided.
- Being careful not to use service to earn admiration from others.
- Having a balance between service and devotional time (Luke 10:38-42).
- Avoiding falling into exhausting and pointless activism.
- Serving others without neglecting the needs of the family.
- Serving others as one would serve Jesus.

Mother Theresa of Calcutta (1910-1997)

Agnes Gonscha Boyaxhiu, better known as Mother Theresa, was born in Albania, Yugoslavia in 1910. Missionaries told Agnes stories of the unhappiness of the people in India, and that moved her heart. At age 12 she knew she wanted to be a missionary in India.

At 18 years of age, she studied English and traveled to India as a missionary. There she worked in a Roman Catholic convent school where there were English and Indian children from wealthy families. Agnes devoted time to learning two local languages: Bengali and Hindi. While doing all of this, she taught poor children on the streets. At age 38, she left the convent where she had served for twenty years to assist the poor on the streets of the city of Calcutta, without any official support or money from her church.

After taking a short course of medicine in Patna, she started to wear a white sari (traditional dress of Indian women) with blue borders, rented a hut in a slum in Calcutta and began to teach poor children. She also bathed the children and sick people, and she shared food with them. Her Indian neighbors, seeing her efforts, gave her some furniture, medicines and school supplies. After two months, 56 children were already attending her school.

But she went further. She went into the poorest part of town, Tijalba, whose streets were full of lepers, abandoned by their families. She then began her fight to create a place where the terminally ill could die in peace. In the meanwhile, many volunteers joined her in her task. Finally, she got two large warehouses located near the temple of the goddess Kali, and she named it "The House of the Dying." There she served people of all religions. Soon the place was filled with children and the sick, so that space and resources became scarce. Mother Theresa sought help from everyone she could so as to continue to assist these people in their need.

Thanks to her example and influence, many centers have been founded in many cities of the world for AIDS patients and for people with other

---

Confirmation questions for the gifts of help or service
• Do I easily identify with the needs of others?
• Do I have a genuine desire to serve others?
• Do I feel satisfaction and joy when I serve others?
• Do I help someone even if it is a sacrifice on my part?
• Do I like to provide assistance to leaders by taking care of details?
• Do I like working "behind the scenes?"

diseases. Mother Theresa received the Nobel Peace Prize in 1979. She died of a heart attack at 87 years of age. She said: "Every act of love, carried out with all the heart, always manages to bring people to God" (Pellini, Claudio 17/12/2009).

The Gift of Hospitality

In this section we will learn what is included in the gift of hospitality.

Scriptures pertaining to the gift of hospitality
Romans 12.3
1 Timothy 5:10
Hebrews 13:21
Peter 4:9

The gift of hospitality is the ability to receive people, house them and make them feel welcome and comfortable, especially those with needs. People with the gift of hospitality find it easy to make friends, and through their testimony, they bring people to Christ. This is an indispensable gift for those who host meetings in their homes. Hospitality should be extended to friends (Proverbs 27:10), other Christians (Galatians 6:10) as well as non-Christian strangers (Leviticus 19:33-34).

Responsibility of people with the gift of hospitality:

- Opening homes to provide shelter and food to people in need.

- Decorating and organizing the surroundings in a way that makes guests feel at home.

- Inviting others to have a meal or a cup of coffee.

- When it is not possible to invite people home, contributing financially to provide housing for those in need.

- Not investing so much in serving others that one's own family is neglected.

- Not confusing Christian hospitality with just being friendly and social.

Frank and Barbara Eby

Missionaries Frank and Barbara Eby arrived in Vietnam as volunteers to teach English in the outskirts of Ho Chi Minch on June 12, 1994. However, their love for the people of Northeast Asia was born many years earlier working for years with thousands of Asian refugees, helping them to settle in the United States while they were members of the First Church of the Nazarene in Tampa, Florida.

While they worked with these Vietnamese families, they opened the doors of their home to receive them and make them feel comfortable. They shared with the immigrants not only their home, but also their money, their time and talents. In addition, Frank was able to start a Nazarene church with these immigrants.

Frank and Barbara sold their house and left everything behind, including their country of origin and their family and friends to make disciples in Vietnam.

Confirmation questions for the gift of hospitality
• Do people enjoy my company?
• Do I look for visitors or individuals in church services so I can make them feel welcome?
• Is it easy for me to talk with a person for the first time and start a new friendship?
• Do I enjoy helping others to make them feel "at home" and well cared for?
• Do I feel deep satisfaction when I open my house to visitors?
• Do I like to plan activities or events that make others feel good?
• Is my stress level low when I receive a guest in my house?
• Am I glad when unexpected guests come to my home?

Lesson 5 - Gifts of Compassion and Service

If these statements apply to you, you may have the gift of generosity.
- I consider it a privilege and not a duty to give money for the work of the church.
- When I give an offering for missions, I always give as much as I can.
- When I see someone in need, I try to provide for the need.
- When I give my tithe, I give more than the minimum and always try to give offerings for special needs.

This passion was awakened in the heart of their daughter, Beverly Wood. She describes the generosity of her parents this way: "My parents would never be successful people in the eyes of the world because they see life through the eyes of Christ and do all they can to heal the wounded around them. Their trophies will never be the material things but the eternal." (Adapted from The Herald of Holiness, Vol 5, No. 139, January-February, 1996).

The Gift of Generosity

In this section we will learn about the gift of giving generously.

The gift of giving can be seen in the desire and ability to contribute with material goods for the needs of others or the work of the Lord. The gift of generosity can be observed in the special disposition to give not only material goods, but also time, talents, and even life itself to fulfill God's will, without expecting anything in return.

Generosity is a practice that has gradually been declining among Christians. In today's world, nobody wants to give something without making a personal profit. When someone gives something for nothing, we are inclined to think that there is an ulterior motive behind it. We have become used to not expecting someone to give us anything out of simple generosity, a desire to help or compassion. Christians with the gift of generosity should help the people of God to make a difference.

Responsibilities of Christians with the gift of generosity

- Sharing generously your time, knowledge and material goods with others (Acts 4:32-37).
- Seeking opportunities to help without expecting anything in return.
- Organizing and motivating others to give generous gifts for missionary work, for projects of the local church, pastoral family, etc.
- Helping everyone equally, without preference.
- Giving generously, but wisely.

Nina Griggs Gunter

Nina Griggs Gunter was born on September 4, 1937, in Bennettsville, South Carolina. She was called to the ministry of preaching at age 14. When she told her pastor about this, he asked her to preach in the next service. Since then she has never stopped preaching. She married Dwight Moody Gunter in 1956 with whom she has two children.

Nina was the first woman to receive an honorary Doctorate of Divinity from Trevecca Nazarene University in recognition of her creative and innovative ministry. In 2005, she was honored by the Nazarene Bible College as "Preacher of the Year." In February 2009, Trevecca awarded her the first Leadership Award in recognition of an exceptional Christian woman who is modeling service and leadership.

As an ordained minister, Nina served as a co-pastor alongside her husband and then as an administrator in the District Office when Dwight served as superintendent (1976-1986). She worked in the ministry of evangelization and as interim pastor of several congregations.

Nina showed her gift of generosity by serving for 35 years as the President of Nazarene Mission International (NMI), first in the District of South Carolina and then beginning in 1986 as the General Director of NMI. Her passionate effort to encourage local churches to have a better vision for missions has led to unprecedented interest and tremendous support. Through her motivation for twenty years, annual world mission offerings increased from $30 million to $62 million, with a total of one billion dollars given to missions.

Dr. Gunter was elected as a member of the General Board of Superintendents at the Twenty-sixth General Assembly in Indianapolis, Indiana, in June 2005. She is the first woman to be honored with that office. The presence of Dr. Gunter on the Board of General Superintendents and her example have enriched the church's global ministry. She was selected as a contributing editor in 2008 and 2009 for the Journal of Leadership of "Christianity Today" because she is one of the most admired church leaders for her faithfulness and the innovative way she has contributed to the mission of Christ in the world (www.nazarene.org/ministries/superintendents/emeritu/gunter/display.html).

Scriptures pertaining to the gift of generosity
Luke 3:11; 21:1-4
John 12:3-8
Acts 4: 32-37; 20:35
Romans 12:8
2 Corinthians 8:2-5

What Did We Learn?

The gifts of compassion, service, support, hospitality and generosity are essential for the church of Christ to show the world the merciful love of God in a tangible and real way.

Activities

Time 20'

INSTRUCTIONS:

1. What are some synonyms for the word compassion?
_____
_____

2. Read the parable of the Good Samaritan in Luke 10:25-37. William Barclay notes three important truths in this story. Write under each truth something you can do this week to implement it.

- We must help a person even if they have caused us harm.

- Any human being of any nation that is in need is our neighbor.

- Our help should be practical and not just in words like "I'm so sorry."

3. Do the following in groups of 3 or 4 students: After reading Luke 22:23-27 answer this question: How can someone with these gifts we have studied in this lesson help the church to fulfill its mission of reaching others for Christ?

4. Application of these gifts in the Church.

The entire class can perform this activity using a large sheet of paper or a blackboard.

The name of each student can be put in the left column. On the right each person should answer this question: What service would you like to provide for the church?

For example, sweeping the sanctuary, putting the chairs away, encouraging members to give offerings, repairing the blackboards in the classrooms, and giving rides to children or the elderly are some possible responses.

Name	Service to be given to the church

Lesson 6

GIFTS RELATED TO CROSS-CULTURAL MINISTRY

Objectives

- List and define the gifts related to cross-cultural ministry.
- Identify the responsibilities of Christians with these gifts.
- Read examples of Christians with these gifts.

Main Ideas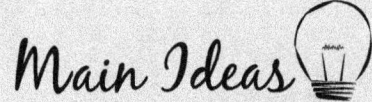

- Apostles fulfilled the purpose of guiding the church and leading its cultural and geographic expansion.
- Missionaries make disciples and fully develop the church in other cultures.

Introduction

The gifts of apostleship, cross-cultural ministry, and language are very important for the extension of the Kingdom of God. Missionaries relate well cross-culturally and are like players on a sports team who have the skills to make points and score goals. They evangelize, plant churches, do social work and are leaders on the mission field. The apostle is someone who takes care of established churches, fulfilling the ministry of guiding the church leaders and missionaries in their work. Their task is similar to a coach on a sports team.

The Gift of Apostleship

In this section we will study the gift of being an apostle.

Jesus taught that all believers share the apostolic mission of the church and have a message to proclaim (John 17:18, 20:21). The gift of "apostleship" is applied to someone sent by God on a mission to preach Christ to the world, plant churches and help them establish themselves; an apostle has special spiritual authority (2 Corinthians 8:23; Philippians 2:25).

The ministry of the apostle is one of the most mentioned in the New Testament. Paul had a special ministry of pastoral care to the spiritual leaders in new churches within the Roman Empire. God and the congregations who sent him to be an apostle gave him the authority to edify the church (2 Corinthians 13:10).

In our days we understand that the gift of apostleship is the desire and the ability to start new groups of Christians, whether in nearby communities, in the city and in rural areas or in other countries and cultures. It is related to the gifts of evangelism, pastoring and leadership.

Responsibilities of a Christian with the gift of apostleship:

- Actively engaging with ministries of evangelism.
- Joining a team of church planters.
- Training at the highest level possible to be a good church planter
- Learning languages that serve as tools for mission.

> In our days, some evangelical churches use the term apostle differently to indicate a high place of leadership in the church. However, the Church of the Nazarene does not use the term in this way, out of respect for the first apostles of the Lord, among other reasons. However, we do understand that leaders who coordinate the work of the servants of the Lord at the district, area, regional, or global levels fulfill a function similar to that of apostle in the New Testament, although the church has chosen not to use this term.

- Participating in volunteer missionary opportunities.

Louie Bustle

Louie Bustle was born in Mount Vernon, Kentucky in 1942. He surrendered to the Lord after the conversion of his father who was an alcoholic. He earned a master's degree in missions at Nazarene Theological Seminary in Kansas City (1982) and Trevecca Nazarene University granted him a Doctorate in Divinity (1987).

He married Ellen Phillips in 1968 and two years later, in 1970, began his missionary service in the Virgin Islands where he worked for four years. In 1975, he began work in the Dominican Republic. There his gift of apostle came to light allowing him to guide churches in tremendous growth up to the point that 61 new churches were organized in six years.

After serving in Peru for a year, in 1983, he was appointed Regional Director for South America. This region, under his leadership, grew from 18 to 40 districts, 375 to 618 organized churches and from 19,300 members to 35,900 in four years.

In 1994, when Dr. Bustle began as the Director of World Mission, the Nazarene Church was present in 104 countries. Since 2009, he has served as the Director of Global Mission for the Church. In 2008, the church already had more than 790 missionaries (in 40 world areas) and over 11,000 volunteers in mission. These missionaries were serving in 148 languages and 75 dialects. By 2009, the Church of the Nazarene was present in 155 countries and of these a third had been started under the ministry of Dr. Bustle.

In the 2010 General Board's report, Dr. Bustle stated: "Ten years ago, the total membership of the Church of the Nazarene was 1.3 million, but now just 10 years later, already well into the 21st century, the century for which God has raised us up, we have more than 600 thousand new members (half of which were received in the last three years), we are positioned to cross the mark of 2 million members at some point during the 2012 calendar year. We celebrate the vitality and strength that we enjoy because of the multitude of gifts that these new Nazarenes bring. The past ten years we have grown by 45%. Just imagine what will happen in the next ten."

Scriptures pertaining to the gift of apostle
Matthew 10:2-15
Romans 16.7
John 13:12-17
1 Corinthians 12:28-29
Acts 8:14-25, 14:14
Acts 15:1-6
2 Corinthians 12:1
Galatians 1:1
Ephesians 4:11

Confirmation questions for the gift of apostle
• Does it make me sad that people do not have a church near their home?
• Do I get excited to participate in the founding of a church?
• Can I identify with the ministry of the apostle Paul?
• Do I admire the work of the missionary church planters?
• Do I feel comfortable working on long-term projects?
• Do I have other gifts of leadership like administration, faith, pastor, etc.?

Gifts for Missionary Service

In this section we will learn about gifts for cross-cultural ministry.

The gift of cross-cultural ministry (missionary) is a special ability that God gives to some members of the body of Christ so they can use their other gifts with people from other cultures. The missionary is willing to cross cultural and social barriers. Paul was an apostle, but he is also an example of a missionary. God called him specifically as a missionary to the Gentiles (Acts 9: 15-16).

Lesson 6 - Gifts Related to Cross-Cultural Ministry

One third of all Nazarene church growth in 2009 was due to the founding of churches:
• 1,178 new churches were founded, which represents 23 new churches each week.
• 165,661 new Nazarenes were added, which is 450 new Nazarenes every day.
• The church reached a total of 24,485 churches globally, with 17,277 of them being organized churches.
• There were 1,900,000 members in total (6% more than in 2008).
(From the Annual Report of the General Superintendents, February 2010)

Scriptures pertaining to the gift of cross - cultural ministry (missionary)
Galatians 1:15-17; 2:7-14
Ephesians 3:6-8; 4:11
Acts 9:13-17; 14:21-28
1 Corinthians 9:19-23

Missionary
The missionary movement of the Church of the Nazarene is more than 100 years old. The doctrine of holiness and missions are at the heart of what it means to be a Nazarene. At the time of the union of holiness groups in Pilot Point, Texas in 1908, the founders had commissioned and sent a total of 21 missionaries to India, Cape Verde, Mexico and Japan. In September 2008, there were 794 missionaries and staff around the world supported by the World Evangelism Fund.

Missionaries are indispensable for the organization of new churches. These are people who joyfully accept God's mission to reach the lost. This gift allows the continuation of evangelistic work through establishing churches in new geographical areas.

Responsibilities of a Christian missionary:

- Being sure that there is a personal call from God to "go and serve in other cultures."

- Cultivating a good relationship with the Lord through a life of prayer.

- Being willing to sacrifice and live without certain things.

- Learning to distinguish and hear the voice of the Holy Spirit.

- Being familiar with the doctrines of the church.

- Receiving training on methods of communication and teaching techniques.

- Learning everything possible about the new culture the missionary is to enter.

- Learning the language of the people of that new culture.

Lucía Carmen García

On November 21, 1919, when she was 15, Carmen Lucia Garcia was the first convert of the Argentine Church of the Nazarene (and probably South America). By the following year Lucia taught in the first Sunday School in Buenos Aires. After graduating as a teacher, she served as principal of the Joint Evangelical School (1923) which began with 23 children. In 1927, she received her certificate of Licensed Minister and began to carry out pioneer work in urban areas in the West of the capital city.

Lucia, assisted by Soledad Quintana, a student of the Bible Institute, started to evangelize along the Sarmiento railroad stations in Buenos Aires. The two got up early every day and went out to evangelize door to door, handing out tracts, and selling Bibles. They ate lunch of bread with cheese and bologna, sitting wherever they could. Lucia preached in crusades sometimes up to for 22 days. As a result of their work there, churches were founded in the cities of Merlo, Castelar, General Rodriguez, Moron, Moreno and other nearby towns, as far away as Lujan (70 km from the center of the capital).

In 1931, both were ordained as elders by Dr. J. B. Chapman. Lucia oversaw the new churches from 1926 until 1939. At the same time, she served as editor of the first Nazarene magazine in Argentina called "La Vía Más Excelente" (The Most Excellent Way) and translated books from English to Spanish. In 1950, while working as a professor at the Bible Institute, she got a Ph.D. in Philosophy.

In 1953, she and her husband Natalio Costa were appointed as the first missionary couple in Argentina with a task to plant churches in the interior provinces of the country. They founded several churches in Tucuman, Santiago del Estero and Salta. A year later, at the 1954 District Assembly, they reported that through personal evangelism and house to house visitation they had distributed 1,053 Bibles, 600 New Testaments, 8,000 portions of Scripture and 80,000 tracts in the city of Tucuman and its surroundings. They had visited hospitals, shops and even the Government Center. Again they shared the gospel along the train routes to reach the neighboring provinces. They started four church plants and trained Sunday school teachers. After a few years they moved to the western provinces where they founded churches in Mendoza and San Juan.

When she was well along in years, Lucia challenged students in the Bible Institute in Buenos Aires with the following words: "We did the job with very little, you have more, do something bigger."

Confirmation questions for the gift of cross-cultural ministry
- Am I attracted to the idea of evangelizing marginalized groups?
- Do I like to do missionary work in other countries?
- Can I adapt well to other cultures?
- Do I have the ease and discipline to learn another language?
- Can I easily start relationships with a stranger?
- Am I willing to use my own resources to fund my travel and expenses?
- Am I willing to work to sustain myself while evangelizing and discipling others?
- Am I a good steward of my financial resources?

The Gift of Language

In this section we will learn about the gift of language.

The gift of interpretation of a language is the ability and skill that the Holy Spirit gives to some Christians to learn a different language so they can use it to edify the church. Without the interpretation of language, we could not understand the sermons, read books or sing songs that were written in a language different from our own. When we understand a message, prayer, hymn or song in another language, it builds and blesses our lives.

Because the New Testament translates the word tongues as both languages and dialects, some Christian churches teach that these "languages" are an unknown language or a prayer language. These Christians interpret speaking in "tongues" as a sign that a person has been filled with the Holy Spirit, and they believe that all Christians should receive this gift. Another interpretation is that some people receive the gift of language to convey a message from God to the church, and in this case there must be another person with the gift of "interpretation of tongues" who can "translate" the message. A passage on which this is based is found in Acts 2:4-6. However, in this event, the purpose was that listeners received the message in their own language or dialect. In fact, as a result some 3,000 people joined the church that day (Acts 2:41).

The Church of the Nazarene has interpreted this gift differently from some of the sister evangelical traditions. Our understanding is that there is a gift of the Spirit that enables certain Christians to speak and interpret languages and dialects.

Nazarenes believe that the sign of a Holy Spirit filled Christian is the fruit of love as taught by the Apostle Paul in Galatians 5:22-23: "But the fruit

Lesson 6 - Gifts Related to Cross-Cultural Ministry

Scriptures pertaining to the gift of language
Genesis 11:1
Acts 2:1-13

Confirmation questions for the gift of language
• Is it easy for me to learn and speak in other languages?
• Do I like to help people who speak different languages to communicate with each other?
• Is it a blessing for me to contribute in the edification of the church?
• Do I feel compassion for people who do not have a Bible and/or books in their own language?

of the Spirit is love, joy, peace, forbearance, kindness, goodness, faithfulness, gentleness and self-control. Against such things there is no law." It is the same holy love of God shown in various forms.

Paul does not mention "speaking in other languages" in his lists, although he was fluent in several languages. He grew up in Tarsus and knew the local dialect. An educated Roman citizen, Paul also spoke Greek. He studied at the Rabbinical School of Jerusalem and thus spoke Hebrew (Acts 22:3). As he traveled throughout the Mediterranean, he must have learned words in local languages while he lived in various cities for months. It is likely that he prayed and preached in several languages. Having said all this, we can say that Paul was a person with the gift of languages. He knew several languages and he used them for the benefit of the body of Christ. In 1 Corinthians 14:18-19 Paul testifies: "I thank God that I speak in tongues (languages) more than all of you. But in the church I would rather speak five intelligible words to instruct others than ten thousand words in an unknown tongue."

Responsibilities of Christians with the gift of language:

- Studying and learning to master more and more languages.

- Being available to act as an interpreter when required.

- For those who enjoy writing, improving writing techniques for correct expression and translations.

- Living a period of time in the country where the language is spoken so as to understand the culture.

- Teaching languages. This can be used as an evangelistic tool.

Hilda's Navarro Testimony

Hilda Elena Garcia Navarro was born in a Nazarene family in Ensenada, Baja California, Mexico in 1969. At the age of seven she gave her life to the Lord and in children's camp, received the fullness of the Holy Spirit.

As a child, because of her father's job, she moved several times around the State of Baja California, which borders the United States. In the border cities, it is common for people to see and hear programs of the American media. As a result she grew up familiar with English but did not necessarily speak it fluently.

At 14, she began to study French and English, the second language (English) at the imposition of her mother. French became a passion for her so she stopped English after a while. The next summer she traveled with the French Alliance to the South of France for intensive courses and in five years she had mastered French. She practically had forgotten English.

The Lord took her to San Diego, California, to attend Point Loma Nazarene University, where she studied journalism and had to learn the details of English grammar. While there she wanted to continue studying French but after taking a placement test, it was recommended that she study another language because she was already very competent in French. She took two years of German, and after graduating from college went to Germany to polish the language at the Goethe Institute in Bonn. When she returned to California, she studied Italian just for fun, but hardly practiced it.

What to her were isolated situations, turned out to be a plan woven by the Master. In 1993, she had the blessing of helping for the first time the international delegates to the General Assembly and Conventions of the Church of the Nazarene, translating for them when necessary. From that time on, she supported church events that required translation of documents and simultaneous interpretation. She has had the privilege of serving brothers and sisters throughout Latin America using the languages that God allowed her to learn.

What Did We Learn?

The gift of apostleship, cross-cultural ministry and language are essential for every generation of Christians to fulfill their mission to make disciples of all families and people of the world.

Activities

Time 20'

INSTRUCTIONS:

1. What is the purpose of the gift of cross-cultural ministry?
_____
_____
_____

2. Indicate which of the following characteristics identify a Christian with the gift of cross-cultural ministry.

- Feels a burden for the lost of other cultures.
- Participates in programs to support international missions
- Feels comfortable evangelizing people as long as they have similar habits.
- Does not like to try different foods.
- Enjoys working with teams of church planters.

3. What is the special ministry that the apostles have and how is it like the ministry of a District Superintendent or Field Strategy Coordinator?
_____
_____
_____

4. Give examples of how people with the gift of apostleship, cross-cultural ministry (missionary) and/or the gift of language can contribute to the local church ministry.

Apostle	Missionary	Language

Lesson 7

Gifts of Creative Arts and Communications

Objectives

- Define the gifts of writing, music, skilled labor, arts and communications.
- Identify the responsibilities of Christians with these gifts.

Main Ideas

- Musicians guide us in worship; communicators serve by connecting ministries and providing support.
- Writers edify God's people and train leaders.
- Artists serve others utilizing their hands to express God's love.

Introduction

Christians with creative gifts remind us of the loving care that God used to create this world with a multitude of colors, sounds, flavors and textures. As will be shown in this lesson, the gifts of writing, music, skilled labor, arts and communications are fundamental to the ministry of the church.

The Gift of Writing

The gift of writing is important in the church.

The gift of writing is the special ability that God gives to certain members of the body of Christ to help them formulate thoughts and ideas to communicate in ways that helps others to find direction, wisdom, knowledge and edification, among other things.

Responsibilities of Christians with the gift of writing:

- Learning to write well using proper grammar, writing and spelling.
- Continually reading and writing to practice these skills.
- Having a good knowledge of theology and Biblical studies.
- Working with the publications of the church or other ministries applying this gift.
- Assisting other leaders to review and edit their writings.

Charles Van Engen

Charles Van Engen was born in 1948 in San Cristobal de las Casas, Chiapas, Mexico. His parents were missionaries. He earned his Masters of Divinity from Fuller Theological Seminary and two doctorates in 1978 and 1981 (PhD) at the Free University of Amsterdam. He served as Youth Pastor in Pasadena, California and later as a missionary in the Presbyterian Seminary of Chiapas. There he developed curriculum and study guides. Among other ministries, he and his wife Jean evangelized in rural areas and they had ministries with university students, with women and they

Confirmation questions for the gift of writing
- Do I prefer to express myself in writing rather than through speaking?
- Do I know many more words than the common person, and I can use them properly?
- Have I written something that has been a blessing to others?
- When I read and find a word I do not know, do I look it up in the dictionary?
- When I write, do I review my material to make sure it is well written?

developed leadership trainings. They also assisted many people when a volcano erupted in northern Chiapas (1981-82). From 1982 to 1985 they coordinated with the 80,000 Mayan refugees that crossed the border into Mexico to escape violence in Guatemala.

Since 1973, Van Engen has given his time to the ministry of education at several seminaries, specializing in missiology. He currently teaches Biblical Theology of Mission and since 1988 has been a member of the faculty of the Intercultural School of Studies at Fuller where he coordinates the doctoral program PRODOLA for Latin America.

Among many other ministries, Van Engen served as President of the General Synod of the Reformed Church in America from 1998 to 1999. He is also the founding president and CEO of Latin American Christian Ministries, Inc.

Since his university days (1966 to 1973), he has always been a passionate writer of books. He has written many books, articles and chapters, and always has a list of new issues on which he wants to write, particularly in the areas of missiology, Bible, mission theology and Latin American studies. He is one of the best-known and most influential missiologists in the church of our time.

His pattern has been:

1. Preach the ideas received from the Lord.

2. Teach these same ideas.

3. Organize the ideas into articles or books.

He never has "written only to write," but wants to share ideas with people whom he has never met. His passion is to call the church to commit to the missionary task.

The Gift of Music

In this section we will learn about the gift of music.

The gift of music is the ability to participate in using our voices or instruments in praise to God. Music is one way we express our worship to God. We use songs to worship privately as well as publically. In the worship service, Christian music includes instrumentation, organization, administration and management; God has given certain brothers and sisters the ability to lead congregations in this special time of sharing together in worship.

Worship: "Worship is the reverence, honor, and service shown to a divine being" (Eby, 2004).

Some people confuse worship with music, but they are not synonyms. Worship is more than music; it is a grateful response to a divine initiative. It is a lifestyle that includes recognition of the sufficiency of God and

Lesson 7 - Gifts of Creative Arts and Communications

dependence on him for our whole life. This is not something to be done only once per week on Sunday. Worship involves our entire life. Jack Hayford said, "Worship is a gift of God to us and is intended to bless and benefit us. God does not need it, we do."

Responsibilities of Christians with the gift of music:

- Living a lifestyle of worship.
- Having private times of worship that parallel the public ministry.
- Not giving more importance to music in the worship service than to the preaching.
- Not thinking of themselves as "stars."
- Taking music lessons and / or singing lessons to perfect the talent given by God.
- Joining a group of church musicians to develop and implement this gift.
- Sharing and teaching this music knowledge to others.
- Studying theology to choose the songs properly.
- Using a balance of styles and rhythms for church programs.

Charles Wesley

Charles Wesley, brother of John Wesley, was born in Epworth, England in 1707. The gifts of the two brothers were complementary. Charles was born premature. His parents wrapped him in a woolen blanket and the baby miraculously survived. Both brothers studied at the University of Oxford. Charles was the one who started the Holy Club that his brother John led. Club members gathered for Bible study, prayer and to examine their spiritual lives; they also gave assistance to the sick, the poor and to prisoners.

Charles was the first of the brothers to experience the full assurance of his personal salvation, on May 21, 1738. The next morning, after meditating on Psalm 107, he composed a hymn of salvation. In 1749, he married Sarah Gwynne. She accompanied the Wesley brothers in their evangelistic journeys throughout Britain, until Charles' health forced them to settle in Bristol in 1765, after serving eighteen years as an evangelist. Charles and Sarah had eight children, but only three survived.

Until the time of the Wesley brothers, the churches sang portions of the Scripture. Charles wrote many hymns, most of which expressed the doctrines of salvation, which they preached and then put to music. His main task was to modernize and improve the old form of religious worship. In bed before his death, he shared his last hymn in 1788. Fifty-six volumes of his hymns were published. Some of the best-known hymns of Charles Wesley are "Jesus, Lover of My Soul," "Hark! the Herald Angels Sing," "O for a Thousand Tongues to Sing," " Love Divine, All Loves, Excelling," "Soldiers

Confirmation questions for the gift of music
• Do you express your worship to God through music?
• When you sing to God do you feel you get "lost" in worship?
• When you sing or pray, does your face reflect how you feel?
• Do you have a good voice and correct pitch?
• When you sing, do you internalize words of the song?
• When you hear others sing, can you easily identify errors?

of Christ, Arise," " Christ the Lord Is Risen Today," "And I am Born to Die" (Soundtrack from the movie *Cold Mountain*). A placard in his home in Bristol says: "His hymns are the possession of the Christian Church."

The Gifts of Skilled Labor and Arts

In this section we will learn about the gifts of skilled work and arts.

The gifts of skilled labor and arts consist of the ability to use different art forms for the work of ministry. There is an infinite range of possibilities from designing bookmarks to building and construction. It covers all types of specializations: drawing, video, crafts, decoration, animation, sewing, cooking, gardening, architecture, carpentry, and the list goes on and on.

Responsibilities for the gifts of skilled labor and arts:

Gift of Skilled Labor	Gift of Arts
Maintenance of buildings and gardens.	Skits, puppets, mime, etc.
Repair or construction of houses.	Decoration for special activities.
Work and witness projects.	Teaching crafts.
Construction of furniture.	Decorating cakes.
Repair of vehicles, etc.	Manufacture and repair of clothing, etc.

Margaret Douglas

Mrs. Margaret Douglas was born in 1924. In 2009 when she was 85, she was a member of the Church of the Nazarene in Belle, West Virginia. In all Margaret participated in 19 Work and Witness trips. A friend commented on a trip she made to Costa Rica.

The 25 team members who traveled stayed in a small room at the Nazarene Seminary of the Americas and began working in the sanctuary of one of the churches in the area of San Jose. At the end of ten days, they were worshiping the Lord in the four walls they had built which replaced a tent. According to Margaret, the building process was difficult because the construction had to be earthquake-proof and all the concrete was mixed by hand.

Margaret's ministry in Costa Rica included cooking and laundry, and when time allowed her she was involved in the construction work. The cooking and the cleaning was a difficult job, starting early in the morning and finishing up after long after dinner. Among the many things she enjoyed were the evening services. After many years, she still remembers the baptism service in a creek and Sunday school classes under the trees.

Confirmation questions for the gift of skilled labor
• Do I feel good about building something with my hands?
• Does it bother me to see the sanctuary and other buildings in disrepair?
• Do I like to share with others as we work together on a project?

Mrs. Douglas has traveled to many places in her experience with Work and Witness such as Guatemala, Chile, Bolivia, Brazil, Kenya, Mozambique, Arizona (Indian Reservation), California (Casa Robles), and Hawaii (construction of a church). One of Mrs. Douglas' favorite trips was to Kenya, but unfortunately she became ill, possibly due to the malaria medication. For three days she could not work. "I was pretty bad physically, but I felt worse because I could not work so I decided that this trip would be the last as I wasn't able to help my team." When she shared this feeling with her team, her friend replied, "I think you will go on the next trip and will be working twice as hard!"

Mrs. Douglas subsequently took part in three more trips, completing her nineteenth trip. She encourages everyone to go on a Work and Witness trip at least once. "Go at once. If you have compassion inside you, you will be ready to go back again."

Confirmation questions for the gift of arts
- Am I creative so as to convey a message in a new way?
- Do I have drawing, designing or acting skills?
- Do I like photography, drawing or graphic design?
- Do I have skills to write dramas and direct actors?

Gift of Communications

In this section we will learn about the gifts related to communications.

The gift of communication consists of the ability to transmit a message effectively. It's not just being able to say something, but doing so in a way that it is received and understood.

Christians with these gifts also need to be able to manage one or more of the different media to communicate the message. These can include but are not limited to the printed page, radio, television and Internet. This gift is also related to the ability to use technology.

Responsibilities of Christians with the gift of communications:

- Striving for excellence in everything.
- Identifying the best way to communicate something and using the appropriate media to transmit the message.
- Being able to guide and advise others with kindness in your area of specialty.
- Working to support other ministries of the church.
- Always having an attitude of service to others.
- Engaging in planning to contribute to others' ideas.
- Staying on top of current technological advances.

Carlos Juárez

Carlos was born in Guatemala in a Nazarene home in July of 1981. He was raised in a village in the north of the country until the age of 10 when the family moved to Guatemala City (capital) because his parents were responding to the call of the Lord. His primary and secondary studies were conducted at the Evangelical Institute America Latina. From a young age he showed a lot of interest in any electronic device that he found. He became interested in computers in 1987 when his family acquired one. From then on, he was interested more and more in learning everything about computers.

During a Christian camp in 1998, at the age of 17, Carlos felt a call in his heart, not to be a pastor or preacher, but to put his talents, gifts and knowledge in the service of God. For some years, in every activity at school, Carlos took photographs and filmed everything he could with a video camera, and then he watched the videos with his friends.

In late 1998, with a quest to put everything he had in the service of God, Carlos became involved as a volunteer in the new ministry of communications that existed in the Regional Office for Mexico and Central America of the Church of the Nazarene (Guatemala City). A missionary who was in charge of the ministry taught him about video production, which later would motivate him to continue in the audiovisual field.

During 1999 he completed a career in electronic engineering, and after that time he realized that his true passion was being behind a video camera. In 2000, he began his B.A. in Radio and Television Production and finished his degree in March 2006.

After several years of serving in the Communications ministry in Guatemala City, Carlos moved to San Jose, Costa Rica in January of 2009 to serve as a missionary where he coordinated the Communications ministry for the Mesoamerican Region.

In 2013, Carlos moved to Argentina with his wife to serve in the ministry of Communications for the South America Region for the Church of the Nazarene.

Carlos says: "I personally believe that God prepares us day by day and the things we do are part of His schooling to use our lives how He wants. God wants us to be happy and to have a full life. He has given gifts to each of us and wants us to use them for Him."

Confirmation questions for the gift of communication
• Am I creative so as to find different ways to communicate an idea?
• Do I want things to go well regardless if the credit is given to someone else? (humility)
• Do I like the idea of using technological tools to communicate something?
• Do I like telling stories in a pleasant and creative way?
• Can I write scripts for radio and television?
• Is it easy for me to use technology or to get familiar with it?
• Do I have the ability to take pictures, record videos, do interviews, as well as other aspects of audiovisual media?
• Do I have skills in the area of computers, networking, software, etc.?

What Did We Learn?

The gifts of writing, music, skilled labor, arts and communications are very important in guiding the church in worship, for advancing of the gospel and the edification of the church in many varied and creative ways.

Lesson 7 - Gifts of Creative Arts and Communications

Activities

Time 20'

INSTRUCTIONS:

1. What do 1 Chronicles 15:20-21 and Nehemiah 12:46 teach about music ministry?
___
___
___

2. In groups of three answer this question: What would happen if we did not have brothers and sisters in our churches with gifts of artistic creativity and communications?
___
___
___
___

3. Applying these gifts to the church

All of the class can take part in this activity. A large sheet of paper or a blackboard will be needed. In the left column, each student writes his or her name and in the right column each person responds to this question: What service could I commit to provide for the church?

Some examples include these: maintenance, join the worship team, collaborating with the projection of the songs, write ads for the newsletter, decorating classrooms etc.

Name	Service to be given to the church

Lesson 8

What Is My Role in the Body of Christ?

Objectives

- Define my calling or passion.
- Identify my work style.
- Find my place of service in the body of Christ.

Main Ideas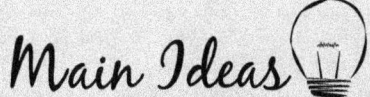

- By identifying my gifts, call and work style, I will be able to better serve the body of Christ.
- In healthy churches, leaders look to each member to serve according to their calling, gifts and style.

Introduction

The apostle Paul describes the Church as the visible body of Christ in this world (1 Corinthians 12:12). The body of Christ works properly when each Christian has a unique and special place of service. Just as in the human body where the organs help each other, the church's spiritual gifts complement each other.

Also, just as the human body is healthy when all its organs and members work well, a healthy church is one where each member is fulfilling their function and building each other up in love (Romans 12).

The purposes for which we serve in the church are to glorify God and edify others. Both should happen together. When a Christian serves others, people can see the glory of God in action and can glorify God by the works He does through His children.

God expects every one of His children to be fulfilled and fruitful in a significant place of service. In addition to identifying your gifts, it is necessary to also identify your passion (call) and work style. A guide to this is included in this lesson.

Our calling and gifts are to enrich the ministry of the church so as to develop a meaningful place of service and in doing so to give glory to God and to serve others.

The churches that develop ministries based on spiritual gifts are healthier and more apt to grow.

How To Find My Role in the Body of Christ?

My place of ministry depends on my gifts, my passion and my style.

To find out the place where God wants you to serve, you have to identify three things: your calling or passion, your gifts, and your personal work style.

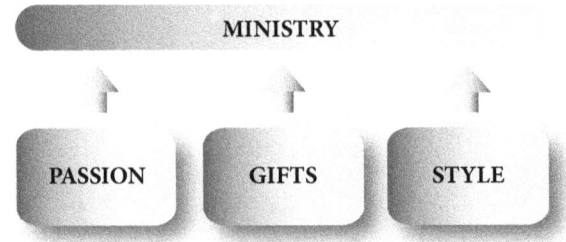

What Is a Call or a Passion?

God calls his children by giving them a special passion.

One Sunday, several church leaders were looking for James. Everyone needed him to meet different needs in their activities for each Saturday of the month. James went home very upset. Because he worked in security for a shopping center, he only had one Saturday off each month and had serious trouble deciding with whom to collaborate. He felt frustrated and guilty about not being able to serve in all those needs. Should he be on the church board because it was his responsibility? Should he support where he could use his artistic skills (decorating the church)? Should he serve doing something where he could feel satisfaction? Should he serve where he was most needed and do something that no one else could?

In the body of Christ, our gifts and passions complement each other.

Have you ever felt like James? The truth is that we can decide to serve in various ministries, but it is much better when we specialize in the area where we have passion.

We can compare the church with an orchestra. In an orchestra there are many instruments: wind, strings, percussion, electronic instruments and several types in each of these categories. It is hard to imagine an orchestra with fifty instruments and six people running from side to side performing a symphony. Some servants of the Lord in the past attempted to do this, and were called "orchestra pastors" meaning they tried to play all the instruments alone.

Just as a symphony is weakened when it uses few instruments, the ministries of the church are weakened when only a few are using their gifts. A healthy and growing church develops many different ministries. The most important responsibility of the leaders according to Ephesians 4:11 is to place each member of the church in a meaningful place of service fulfilling their gifts and passion (call).

When members are serving according to their calling, they do not mind getting up early, they serve with more joy, they encourage others, they impact peoples' lives, and they are dedicated. They strive to do things with excellence, and they will invest their own money to enable them to achieve that task!

God calls us all to serve
Galatians 5:13
Hebrews 10:25
2 Corinthians 9:7
Acts 1:8
1 John 4:1
Titus 2:4
1 Corinthians 12:25

The apostle Paul discovered that the real purpose of his life was to preach the gospel to the Gentiles. His passion was such that he said: "...Woe to me if I do not preach the gospel" (1 Corinthians 9:16). His call was so powerful that if he did not do it, his life would be meaningless.

In the church we all have gifts and we all need to serve. Some people describe it as a "calling." There are those who discover it by a dream or a vision. The passion to invest in something that we consider valuable is a necessity or inner motivation that God puts in us to guide and help us to fulfill His purpose.

Lesson 8 - What Is My Role in the Body of Christ?

How Do I Identify My Passion (My Call)?

The thing that most motivates me is my passion.

To discover your passion, you must identify what motivates you. That depends on what you think is the most important issue that God calls you to devote your life to. A Christian can feel passion for people, for tasks or for a cause.

If what motivates you is people, you will feel inclined to work with a specific group of people: single mothers, children with disabilities, the terminally ill, adolescents, couples, the elderly, prisoners, hospitalized people, among others.

If what motivates you are tasks, then you will feel it important to perform a function that solves a problem or meets some need in the church. This could include being a preacher, administrator, counselor, teacher, writer, driver, missionary, cook, etc.

If you feel passionately about a cause, then you must identify it. Examples of causes include education for poor children, homes for people affected by natural disasters, enacting pro-life laws, dissemination of the Word by mass media, improvement of work conditions, etc.

Felicity was very concerned about the unhealthy ways in which mothers were feeding their children and the lack of exercise by children in her community. She had studied how to eat well and have a healthy life. She could talk for hours on this issue and seems not to tire of it. She has a collection of clips from magazines, many books on the subject and has read almost all there is on the topic. Often she prays that God would have mercy on these children. She recently discovered that she has the gift of teaching.

What is Felicity's passion? It is the health of children. So, she could join the ministry of Compassion in her local church. Her gift is teaching. She can serve by teaching parents, teachers and children about how to eat healthily and the importance of incorporating physical activity in their daily lives.

Charles has been a member of the church for 15 years. He has the gift of administration and has long served as treasurer of his local church. The needs of pastoral families in his district touch his heart. He often seeks the opportunity to discuss the needs of the pastoral families and the lack of concern that has been observed in the churches. Charles has a passion for a cause: improving living conditions for pastoral families. Charles could serve by helping churches to be more fair, responsible and generous to their pastors and to help churches practice good stewardship.

In the Activities section there is a test to identify your passion.

My passion indicates WHERE I should serve.

Passion is a God-given desire that is in the core of our being that prompts us to invest in a particular ministry. The call is for life. "... for God's gifts and his call are irrevocable" (Romans 11:29).

How Do I Identify My Personal Work Style?

We all have different preferences as to how to work.

The personal work style is represented by the preferences that each one has in relating to others. Have you ever wondered: Why do I enjoy concentrating on one task, but not another? Why am I realistic and my friend is a dreamer? Why is it so hard to clean my room? Why do I like to chat more with my friends than do homework? Why do I prefer to run the sound system instead of welcoming visitors at the services?

The answer to all these questions is the same. We all have preferences about what we do and how we relate to people. It is very important to identify personal styles so we can serve in the church with more enthusiasm.

Henry has two tasks in Sunday school. He is responsible to purchase the materials, and he is also in charge of games with the children. Often when he shops for materials he can't concentrate well and almost always forgets something.

He wishes that someone else could take care of this. In contrast, when he is playing with children, time "flies." In fact, if it were up to him, he would spend every day with the children. Why is Henry not equally comfortable in both tasks? This is because he feels more comfortable working "with" the people rather than performing tasks "for" people.

Theresa is in charge of the decoration for special activities and she is also the church secretary. When finishing doing a decoration, Theresa feels at peace with herself because she has finished her work. When she has to update the membership list or the documents and files, she is discouraged to see the papers that accumulate on her desk constantly. Theresa dislikes routine tasks that seem never ending.

What happens to Theresa? Why doesn't she feel the same enthusiasm for both tasks? The answer is that Theresa feels comfortable with variety, doing those tasks in which she can be spontaneous, but she does not have the same desire for tasks where she has to follow an administrative process.

Henry and Theresa need to serve in tasks which correspond to their personal work style.

To identify the personal work style you must ask yourself these questions: What motivates me? Completing tasks for people or working directly with people? How do I organize? Am I structured or spontaneous? In the Activities section, there are exercises to identify your work style.

Personal work style indicates HOW I serve.

Personal work style is related to personality and temperament and is as unique as a fingerprint. God has created each person with these characteristics; therefore, we should not hide them. We should identify them so we can find the place where we can best serve others for the glory of the Lord.

How Do I Get Started Serving in a Ministry?

Do not worry if your passion is not related to a ministry that already exists in your church. God can use you to start a new ministry.

Good leaders begin as apprentices.

The first thing needed is to find a possible field of service. This will depend on gifts, passion and work style.

Here is an example:

	Martha	**Jonah**	**Vincent**
Same GIFT	TEACHING		
Different PASSION	OLDER ADULTS	COUPLES - MARRIAGE ENHANCEMENT	ADOLESCENTS
Style	Structured Tasks	Unstructured with People	Structured with People
Possible areas of service	- Lead Bible studies at home - Write lessons	-Direct dynamics in camps - Talk at weekend events	- Leading a Bible study group - Teaching Sunday School classes

When we place people to serve in a ministry for which they do not feel passion, the result is disinterest, reluctance, resignation, irresponsibility and lack of motivation. On the other hand, you can see the difference when people serve in a minstry they are passionate about.

Martha, Jonah and Vincent have the same gift of teaching. However, their passions and styles are different. Martha and Vincent are structured so they can serve in specific ministerial functions, which work within a team of a determined group of people (formal relations). Moreover, Jonah and Vincent served in tasks that involve working directly with people, where their relationships are spontaneous (ministering to people who are new to them). Martha and Vincent serve in a more structured and permanent ministry. Jonah is the only unstructured person and therefore can serve in generic functions to support the marriage ministry in his church.

Here is another example:

God confirms our gifts and our passion as the people we serve are edified.

	Roger	**Mary**	**Pauline**
Same PASSION	MINISTRY TO SINGLE MOTHERS		
Different GIFT	Administration	Service	Generosity
Style	Structured Tasks	Unstructured with People	Structured with People
Possible areas of service	- Plan courses for single mothers - Coordinate a daycare	-Take care of the kids while the mothers work - Train people to look after children	- Coordinate fundraising events - Coordinate a sponsorship program

School of Leadership - Discovering My Vocation in Christ

Roger, Mary and Pauline have the same passion for helping single mothers, but they have different gifts and styles. Roger and Pauline, who are more structured, serve in roles that require planning, organization and coordination. However, Mary serves in tasks that do not need too much advanced planning.

To start serving, the first step is to join a ministry team. The best leaders are those who start with the simplest tasks and over time increase responsibility. For example, a Christian called to teach could serve as an assistant teacher, and as he or she learns and receives training, he or she can be assigned more responsibilities. Then, with time and practice, this teacher can become the lead teacher of a class. Christian leadership includes the continual training of "apprentices."

The ministry in the church is an endless chain of leaders who train others to lead. To begin, we learn from a mature Christian with more ministerial experience, and then we begin to train others with our example and experience.

How Do I Prepare To Serve in a Ministry?

Preparation is a key element for successful ministry.

The preparation for service is very important. This training must be comprehensive. First, general knowledge that is common to all ministries must be learned, but equally important is the specific knowledge needed to serve on a church ministry team: Discipleship, Sunday School, Leadership, Compassion, Cross-cultural Missions, Evangelism, and Communications, among others.

Second, preparing to serve requires learning practical skills which are acquired "on the job": observing leaders, listening to testimonies or work reports, and performing a task. This is known as experiential learning (1 Timothy 4:15-16, 2 Timothy 1:6-7 and 2:15).

Third, it requires growing in Christian maturity, which is an indispensable quality to serve in a ministry. Christian maturity means growing into the image of Christ, being more like Jesus every day. We need to learn to think like Him, to love like Him, to live like Him, to serve like Him and to relate to others like Him. When we serve, we are models for others and share what God has given us. Growth as a servant implies growth in one's personal relationship with Christ.

The program of the School of Leadership is designed to help disciples to be trained for the ministry to which God has called them.

If everyone were interested in serving in the same ministries, there would be many needs neglected.

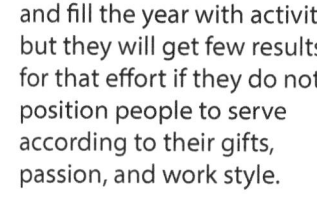

Pastors and leaders can have a lot of passion for the lost and fill the year with activities, but they will get few results for that effort if they do not position people to serve according to their gifts, passion, and work style.

What Did We Learn?

To find the place of service in the body of Christ, we must identify our gifts, our passion and work style. My passion indicates where I can serve, and my personal work style indicates how I can serve. To serve we have to be trained, and we can start by joining a ministry team as an apprentice.

Lesson 8 - What Is My Role in the Body of Christ?

Activities

Time 20'

INSTRUCTIONS:

1. To identify your passion, answer the following questions:

What do you think is the most important thing in which you can invest your time?

What things would you like to be remembered for after your death?

What do you feel such a passion for that you could spend hours talking about it?

When you imagine your "ideal" future, what do you see yourself doing in 5 or 10 years?

Of the things you have done and are proud of, which one or ones did you enjoy the most?

What are those activities that make you lose track of time?

Have you ever felt when you were serving that you were doing exactly the will of God? What were you doing?

Summarize your passion in one sentence: MY PASSION IS _____.

2. Identify your personal work style:

In the two tables below, choose the description that is closer to your preference by placing an "x" in either the left or right column. Then add the number of "x" at the bottom of each column.

Am I motivated by tasks?	X	Am I motivated by people?	X
I feel satisfied when I finish a task		I feel satisfied when I spend time with a person	
When I work directly with people I feel exhausted		When I have to do administrative tasks I feel exhausted	
I can concentrate for a long period of time on a task		I can't concentrate for a long period of time on the same task	
If I meet a friend, I greet him quickly and arrive on time for my meeting		If I meet a friend, I may stay talking and be late for my meeting	
I prefer to prepare a program		I prefer to run a program	
I like dealing with the details behind the scenes		I feel comfortable working directly with people	
I like to specialize in one task		I like to develop relationships with people	
It motivates me to finish a task		It motivates me to make friends	
The most important thing is to reach my goals		The most important thing is to take care of people	
My holidays include doing something new and different, in a place with few people (like fishing, reading, etc..)		My favorite break is to be with family or friends or in a place where I can meet people, to talk, play, etc..	
Motivated by tasks		**Motivated by people**	

Am I a structured type of person?	X	*Am I a spontaneous type of person?*	X
Before going to the supermarket I make a list		I go to the supermarket without a list	
Functions that demand a permanent commitment motivate me.		I prefer short-term work projects	
I feel comfortable when working with a plan		I feel comfortable when working in a spontaneous way	
I like a routine		I feel comfortable with variety	
Before starting work, I put my desk in order		At work, I put my desk in order only when necessary	
I like long term goals		I like to see quick results	
If I was a musician, I would play by reading music		If I were a musician I would play by ear	
A scheduled meeting must start on time		I start the meeting when there is a good group of people in attendance	
I plan my vacations ahead of time and organize everything I'm going to take so I don't forget anything		I go on vacations when I can. I pack at the last minute and if I forget something, I pick it up later	
Structured		**Spontaneous**	

3. To identify where I can begin to serve:

My specialty ministry is _____

My strongest gifts are _____

My passion is _____

My work style is

    Structured: _____   Spontaneous: _____

What motivates me the most are

    Tasks: _____   People: _____

Some possible areas of service for me would be: _____

4. *How do I prepare myself to serve? Mark with an "x" one or two specialties of the School of Leadership that could assist you as you seek to serve in your church.*

    1. MINISTERIAL LEADERSHIP _____   *5. CROSS-CULTURAL MISSIONS* _____

    2. EVANGELISM _____   *6. COMPASSIONATE MINISTRY* _____

    3. CHRISTIAN DISCIPLESHIP _____   *7. COMMUNICATIONS / LITERATURE* _____

    4. YOUTH MINISTRIES _____

Final evaluation

Time 15'

COURSE: DISCOVERING MY VOCATION IN CHRIST

Name of Student: _____
Church or Study Center: _____
District: _____
Professor / Course: _____
Date of this evaluation: _____

1. Complete the following sentences:

My specialty ministry is: _____
My strongest gifts are: _____
My passion is: _____

My work style is: Structured: _____   Spontaneous: _____
What motivates me the most are: Tasks: _____   People: _____

2. According to previous answers, some possible areas of service for me would be these:
_____

3. The specialty course(s) of the School of Leadership that would help me to better prepare myself to serve in my church is/are:

1. MINISTERIAL LEADERSHIP   5. CROSS-CULTURAL MISSIONS
2. EVANGELISM   6. COMPASSIONATE MINISTRIES
3. CHRISTIAN DISCIPLESHIP   7. COMMUNICATIONS / LITERATURE
4. YOUTH MINISTRIES

4. Explain how this course helped you to identify and assess your spiritual gifts, passion, and work style.
_____
_____
_____

5. What did you learn through the ministerial practice activities in this course?
_____
_____
_____

6. In your opinion, how could this course be improved?
_____
_____
_____

Bibliography

Books:

Ahleman, Dorotea. *Bodas de Oro 1979-1969 Distrito Argentino.* Buenos Aires: Church of the Nazarene, 1970.

Boyer, Orlando. *Biografia de grandes cristianos. Vol. 2.* Miami, Florida: Vida, 1983.

Bugbee, Bruce. *Cuál es tu lugar en el cuerpo de Cristo. Descubre tus dones espirituales, tu estilo personal y la pasión que Dios te ha dado.* Miami: Vida, 2001.

Deiros, Pablo. *Los dones del Espíritu Santo.* Buenos Aires: Fundación Argentina de Educación y Acción Comunitaria, 2004.

Eby, J. Wesley; Lyons, George and Trusdale, Al. *A Dictionary of the Bible and Christian Doctrine in Everyday English.* 2nd Edition, 2004.

Hurn, Raymond W. *Descubra su ministerio.* Guatemala, C. A.,: CNP, 1878.

Jay, Ruth I. *Cristianos Intrépidos. Vol 2.* Quito, Ecuador, The Good News Broadcasting Association, Inc.: 1984.

Kuen, Alfred. *Dones para el servicio.* Barcelona: CLIE, 1993.

Price, J.M. *Jesús el Maestro.* El Paso, Texas: CBP., s/f.

Purkiser, W.T. *Los dones del espíritu.* Kansas City: CNP, 1979

Schwarz, Christian. *Método para la prueba de dones.* España: CLIE, 1994.

Smith, Ebbie. *Descubra sus dones espirituales.* E.U.A.: CBP, 1981

Vine, W.E. *Diccionario Expositivo.* Grupo Nelson, 2007.

Wagner, Peter. *Sus dones espirituales pueden ayudar a crecer a su iglesia.* España: CLIE,1980.

Woodbridge, John D. Ed. *Grandes Líderes de la Iglesia.* Miami: Vida, 1998.

Young, José. *Los dones del Espíritu.* Córdoba, Argentina: Ediciones Crecimiento Cristiano, 1998.

Magazines:

Revista El Heraldo de Santidad. *Dejar todo por los que tienen poco.* En Volumen 50, Número 139. Enero-Febrero 1996. pp. 30-31. Nazarene Publishing House, Kansas City, Missouri.

Web Pages:

Board of General Superintendents, Church of the Nazarene "Dr. Nina Griggs Gunter." *Official site of the International Church of the Nazarene.* Updated August 2013. Accessed September 19, 2013. http://nazarene.org/ministries/superintendents/emeriti/gunter/display.html

Burnis, Bushong. (2008). *Juan Wesley, Un hombre con un mensaje.* Recuperado el 22 de Octubre de 2008 de: www.wesleyana.org/RECURSOS/HISTORIA/JUANW/JWmensaje.pdfel.

Centro Online de Juan Wesley (2008). Recuperado el 20 de Octubre de 2008 de: http://wesley.nnu.edu/espanol/

Mujer Valiosa Tv. (2008). Recuperado el 17 de Noviembre de 2008 de: http://www.mujervaliosa.com/tv_liliana.html

Smalling, Roger L. El liderazgo cristiano. Manual para el curso sobre el libro en internet: Recuperado 15 de mayo 2009 de: http://www.smallings.com/LitSpan/Manuales/LiderazgoEspiritual.htm/

Wikipedia. La enciclopedia libre. "James Dobson" consultado el 23 de Febrero de 2010. http://es.wikipedia.org/wiki/James_Dobson

Como oraban Tomo 2 Oraciones de ministros. Recuperado 1 marzo 2010 de: http://www.elcristianismoprimitivo.com/comoorabancap8.htm

Pellini, Claudio. Planeta Sedna. Portal de difusión de la historia. Madre Teresa de Calcuta. Recuperado 2 de marzo 2010 de: http://www.portalplanetasedna.com.ar/teresa.htm. Última actualización 17-12-2009.

www.ingramcontent.com/pod-product-compliance
Lightning Source LLC
Chambersburg PA
CBHW080941040426
42444CB00015B/3399